D0615927

Re-creating
THE
Church

Re-creating THE Church

COMMUNITIES OF EROS

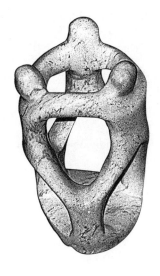

Pamela Dickey Young

TRINITY PRESS INTERNATIONAL
Harrisburg, Pennsylvania

Copyright © 2000 Pamela Dickey Young

All rights reserved. No part of this book may be reproduced, stored in a retrieval system, or transmitted in any form or by any means, electronic, mechanical, including photocopying, recording, or otherwise, without the written permission of the publisher, Trinity Press International.

Trinity Press International
P.O. Box 1321
Harrisburg, PA 17105

Trinity Press International is a division of The Morehouse Group.

Cover design by Trude Brummer

Library of Congress Cataloging-in-Publication Data

Young, Pamela Dickey, 1955-
    Re-creating the church : communities of eros / Pamela Dickey Young.
      p. cm.
    Includes bibliographical references and index.
    ISBN 1-56338-320-9
      1. Church. 2. Feminist theology. I. Title.

BV600.2 .Y685 2000
230'.082-dc21   00-026715

Printed in the United States of America

00 01 02 03 04 05   10 9 8 7 6 5 4 3 2 1

For Carol—
who has taught me a lot about flourishing
and right relationship

Contents

Acknowledgments

Books take on a life of their own as they come into being. I did not know until I was well into thinking about the ideas that became this book that it would be a book about ecclesiology. What began as a set of questions about how North Americans are religious at this point in time and why they do not seem to be looking to belong to traditional religious institutions as a way of expressing that religiosity became a book about the sort of institutional religiosity I know best, the Christian churches. My niggling worries about how churches are failing religious seekers became extended reflections on how this could be different.

Portions of this book were given as the Pond Lectures at Bangor Theological Seminary in January 1998. Another portion was given as a lecture at New College, University of Edinburgh in May 1999. My sincere thanks to those who listened and raised good questions about my ideas and intentions.

My class on women and religion in 1998–99 helped me think about what today's central religious questions are as the students shared their own religious questions with me. I discussed the development of this book with my class on church and sacraments in the winter of 1999. They offered feedback and many fine insights, some of which are incorporated here.

Thanks to many colleagues and friends, in particular to Carol Allison-Burra, Ellen Goldberg, Cliff Hospital, Hal Llewellyn, and Jean Stairs for their encouragement and for their willingness to talk with me about various topics relevant to the book.

Thanks to Henry Carrigan and Laura Hudson at Trinity Press International for their interest in this project and for their editorial expertise. Thanks also to Linda Thomas for her "eagle eye" in proofreading and preparing the index.

I am grateful to McClelland and Stewart, Inc. for their permission to reprint a quotation from Margaret Laurence; to Jeremy Baxter for permission to reprint a quotation from Bronwen Wallace; and to *Theological Studies* for their permission to use in chapter 3 portions of an article first published there.

Introduction

Can churches find new ways of being when old ways no longer seem to fit? What if we began to think of churches as communities of eros (that is, communities where love entailed connection and passion) rather than communities of agape (that is, communities where love is said to be all giving and no receiving, allowing for no real connections)? What if we constructed church life based on that vision? These are the questions that underlie this book.

I did not think that I would ever write a book about the church. This book began as a book about religious searching at the turn of the millennium, but I soon found myself hoisted on my own feminist contextual petard because my first thoughts were too generic. I realized that I could not write a book about everyone's search. Yet, having thought about the search, I was pushed by my own contextuality and commitments to think about ways in which this search finds satisfaction. I was pushed to look at the Christian church, because this is the context in which I have the most experience and knowledge for serious reflection.

Like most feminists who have tried to stay within a religious tradition rather than find other options, I have a love-hate relationship with the church. On the one hand, the institutional churches have been perpetrators of women's oppression in a variety of ways. Yet, on the other hand, many feminist women have been reluctant to leave because they think and experience things that are worth transforming.

In my own case, I navigated that problem with the institutional church in a couple of ways. First, I had the good fortune to be raised in a denomination, The United Church of Canada, where women have been ordained since 1936 and where justice concerns have always been a main focus. Second, instead of worrying too

1

much about the institution, I concentrated on theology. That is, as a theologian I thought that one could reconceive and reconstruct Christian theology in ways that countered oppression, and I thought that if I spoke—and many others like me, of course—the church would follow theology.

But I kept teaching class after class of entering theological students who were intent on church ministries but who had never in their lives in the church encountered feminist critique of church and theology. And class after class of university undergraduates in religious studies saw the church as the problem, not as part of the solution to any religious or social questions they might have. For them, churches could not be agents of transformation. Yet these students had religious questions: about meaning, about values, about transcendence, about connection to the universe.

Thus, this project is born of four sources: first, the questions of my students; second, my conviction that Christian theology can and ought to be a force for change; third, my concern that churches are not responding to the critiques that feminists and others have made in ways that would make them liberating or transformative forces; and fourth, my concern about what appears to be the individualism of so much of contemporary North American life that removes many from communities of affiliation, leaving them potentially solitary and solipsistic.

I am writing from my North American, specifically Canadian, context. Others will have to say if any of this applies in other settings. Ecclesiastically, we are living in changing times, when the old strategies for ways to be the church seem not to be working.[1] We do not really expect the once-mainline churches to grow, but we do not know how to deal with decline. We worry that the average age of churchgoers is increasing, but we have no sense of what might attract others to the church.

One of the things that became clearer to me as I was writing this book was that if there is hope for the church, that hope rests much more in congregations than in larger groupings such as denominations or in "the church" as a whole. If change of the sort that I am advocating is to happen, it will begin at the grass roots. Thus, churches, denominations, and congregations, especially those who want to speak to contemporary concerns, need to do a better job than they have done of showing that not all churches are the same, that there is no monolithic church.

My interest in this question is more theological than sociological. That is, my interest is in how Christian churches, at the turn of the millennium, can define and understand themselves in relation to the historical Christian tradition and to contemporary questions and contexts. I am very clear that not all parts of the Christian church will want to engage in such a task. One of the things that I have learned from feminism is that what appears to be monolithic from a distance rarely is that when seen up close. The closer we get to the church, the more diversity we can see. So, my interest is in those parts of the church that do want to think about change. If we really do want to change the church, at least at a congregational level, to meet some of the critiques that are being leveled against it, what are some of the things we need to be thinking about?

In the first chapter of this book I discuss how I think late twentieth-century North American religious searching might best be described. I settle on the terms *flourishing* and *right relationship* as ways to discuss what human beings seem to be looking for. And I consider the capacity for transcendence that makes religious questioning possible.

Then I turn to some of the ways the church has inhibited flourishing and right relationship. Here I discuss such problems as fear of embodiment and sexuality, which has traditionally also led to fear or denigration of women as more representative of these qualities than men. Fear of sexuality has also led to heterosexism. The question whether churches will accept women or gay members as leaders is an important challenge. I raise the concern regarding traditional alliances of churches with ruling powers. I ask about the relationship of churches to the ecological crisis and to various religious traditions. I also raise the question of theological interpretation. Have some of our theological interpretations and concepts outlived their usefulness as illuminations of religious life? Have we been dragged into a false theological literalism by insisting on only one interpretation of what may well be polyvalent religious symbols?

One of my interests is a specifically feminist one. Can churches be places of flourishing and right relationship for women as well as men, and for women and men together? What gets in the way of such flourishing? What might aid it?

I look to Christian churches as one possibility for fostering flourishing and right relationship not because I think Christianity, or its institutional forms in the Christian churches, is the only or even the most likely place to encounter such fostering. Indeed, the challenges that I have alluded to only briefly might make one wonder if one should bother with the church at all. Yet, for reasons that are born both of my own experience in the church and of my theological thinking about what the church could and should be, I think there are resources that churches are not fully using that, if developed, could be forces in the flourishing and right relationship that many people are seeking. From another perspective, I think that if the church is to survive into the twenty-first century as a meaningful institution rather than as a sociopolitical anachronism, churches must begin or continue to attend to some of the challenges that have been mentioned.

The church is not monolithic. The church is made up of very diverse denominations that vary not only because of denominational history but also because of their contextual situations in time and place. In addition, within denominations there are many varied individual congregations who take part of their identity from their denominational background but who exist in their own sometimes stunning individuality.[2] This individuality may be fostered or hampered by various denominational structures and authorities. Here, even though I occasionally talk about the church in the singular, I am mindful that individual denominations and congregations are varied and variable.

In the second chapter I present a theological vision of church as *a diverse collection of communities of eros who find their common identity in the shared memory and presence of Jesus Christ and seek to embody God's transforming grace by fostering flourishing and right relationship for all creation.* I unpack this vision piece by piece as a way to illuminate what I take to be of central importance in understanding church. It is my conviction that as a theological ideal, the vision of church that I present here is one that could serve churches well if they truly are seeking to be Christian churches and to meet religious needs at the turn of the millennium.

This interpretation as I present it is not everybody's vision of the church. As much as I would like the "church universal" to become what I think is needed and what I think it has the potential to be, I don't think this will happen. There are too many competing visions of the church motivated by too many competing interests for such universality to be possible ever again. The only way a singular view of the church would define all is to ignore the diversity that already exists and weed out those whose diversity goes "too far" from the legislated norms.[3] But I do think that this vision of the church as I present it could be the aim or ideal of some churches. I am interested in whether churches can be saved from irrelevance by adopting new ways of thinking and being.

After looking at each piece of the definition, I turn to resources that churches have at their disposal that would help them come closer to this vision, that would enable them to meet current needs while fulfilling the impetus that called them into existence. I look at preaching and teaching, at ritual, at personal and community formation, at social action as places where the church can attend to the enacting of this vision.

The subtitle of the book, *Communities of Eros*, comes from the first phrase in my definition. The meaning and import of this subtitle will, I hope, become clear as the argument of the book progresses. Here, then, I want only to offer a few comments by way of setting the stage. The argument of the book begins in an attempt to focus on human need or desire and on how religious communities might meet that need or desire, as well as on some of the issues that have arisen as churches have failed to respond to what is needed. For the purposes of this book, I have named the desire and its needed solution as eros. In using the term *eros* to describe a vision of the church, I mean to claim that passion and connection ought to be central to churches' self-understandings and ways of acting in the world, and I situate this passion and connection within the historical Christian tradition.

Here I present one vision of church that I hope will illuminate and challenge.

NOTES

1. See Douglas John Hall, *The Future of the Church: Where Are We Headed?* (Toronto: The United Church Publishing House, 1989), 1–22; and Nancy Tatom Ammerman, with Arthur E. Farnsley II et al., *Congregation and Community* (New Brunswick: Rutgers University Press, 1997), 45.

2. This is clearly what Ammerman found in her study of a variety of congregations adapting to change. See Ammerman, *Congregation and Community*.

3. For example, on Sunday, June 13, 1999, Time/CNN broad-
cast a show about a parish in Rochester, New York, that was excom-
municated from the Roman Catholic Church for having a woman
perform in liturgical roles that go beyond what the Roman Catholic
Church will sanction. The parish continues to meet and to think of
itself as a Roman Catholic parish, but the church has "weeded out"
this diversity.

1. Being Religious at the Turn of the Millennium

Human Searchings

The undergraduate students that I teach ask profoundly religious questions. They worry about the state of the earth and themselves in it. They worry about where they fit in the universe and how they can be meaningfully connected with the whole as well as its parts. I am interested in their searches and in whether there are any ways to talk about human searching that illuminate human religiosity more generally and yet still take account of the contexts in which people live—contexts that shape their lives, the questions they ask, and the answers they find acceptable to those questions.

Human searching has taken many and various forms. Whether or not there is anything like a universal human search is much in dispute as scholars, for a variety of reasons, have shied away from the essentialism that it implies.[1] Talk of what it means to be human takes place in the concepts of the one doing the talking. Can we really transcend our socio-cultural-historical locations if our language is tied to those locations? Privileged Western, middle-class, male, white scholars have often ignored everyone's reality but their own, meaning that the diversity of humanity has not been, until recently, listened to or noted in its full force. To talk about human searching, then, means to talk about this searching from one time and place to see if it rings true for others.

Here I am interested in the kind of searching that is often called "religious." There is no single definition of religion that is agreed upon by all scholars, but for my purposes here, William P. Alston's "religion-making characteristics" serve to show the general breadth of religion:

1. Belief in supernatural beings (gods).
2. A distinction between sacred and profane objects.
3. Ritual acts focused on sacred objects.
4. A moral code believed to be sanctioned by the gods.
5. Characteristically religious feelings (awe, sense of mystery, sense of guilt, adoration)
6. Prayer and other forms of communication with gods.
7. A worldview, or a general picture of the world as a whole and the place of the individual therein.
8. A more or less total organization of one's life based on the worldview.
9. A social group bound together by the above.[2]

By religious questions, then, I mean questions that arise from one or more of the characteristics above—questions, for example, about the gods (I would say transcendence); about values; about how the universe is organized and where one fits in it, and so on.

Certainly my own view of what humans are searching for and how religious traditions provide symbolic guidance in that search is colored by my own search, which is without question affected by my own social-historical-political location.

I grew up in a mainline Protestant church in rural Canada. The church provided a focus for certain community activities and, therefore, met certain social needs. Because much of my church activity was music-related, the church also met some of what I later began to see as aesthetic needs. Early on I was skeptical of the church both as a provider of moral guidance and as an answerer of the religious questions that I had begun to ask. In particular, as a teenager I found the church intellectually bankrupt, asking me, I thought, to believe the incredible without argument or hesitation. As a person of very-much-modern sensibilities, I was not about to believe anything without rational justification.

When I went to university, therefore, my first thought was that I had now "outgrown" the church. But there was a vital worshiping community at the university I had chosen and a minister in the local congregation who was willing to address difficult theological issues. These, combined with an introductory course in biblical studies, led me to begin to see that there were ways to combine my intellectual needs for credibility with responsible biblical criticism and theological interpretation. I stayed in the church because religious issues were important to me: I needed to struggle with questions about who I was in relation to God (or whatever passed as ultimate) and how I should live in response to that. When I discovered that thinking people had asked these difficult questions before me, I realized that the church at least held out the possibility of meeting my intellectual/rational needs. Furthermore, it gave me a community of people to relate to long before I identified myself with the academic community that would become my permanent home.

I never expected nor allowed the church to be the sole arbiter of moral decision making. Undoubtedly, the Maritime Canadian culture, pervaded as it was by a certain ethos of Protestantism, was an influence on the moral world in which I grew up. As I further explored the religious questions that were arising for me, I began to see that certain answers to these questions were tied to certain moral attitudes, if not directly, then by way of influence one on the other. When I was in theological college, I discovered feminism and the import of its questions for the church. I realized that if I were going to continue to be part of the church, it would also have to hold out the possibility of taking women seriously. I was lucky enough to have been born into Canada's most liberal denomination . . . the United Church of Canada, which had been ordaining women since the 1930s, so the first and most crucial question about my participation as a woman in the church had been dealt with. By the time I discovered that the questions of feminism went far beyond the matter of ordination, I had decided to stay within the church to try to change it from the inside.

It is only in retrospect that I realize that one of the reasons I continued to be part of the church was aesthetic—in particular, through music, both in my own music making and in my appreciation for the music of the church. Even though the music of the church of my youth is not the music that I would now choose, church was one of the few places where I grew up that one could participate in the musical enterprise.

My current location is still as an insider to the church: an ordained woman and an academic, whose passion for the intellectual questions took her to graduate school and a life in teaching; a woman who is committed to rigorous intellectual thinking about theology, but who also sees that thinking is profoundly connected to life as lived and vice versa.

My attachment to Christianity has consistently been one that
sees that the institutional church does not always embody the best
that can be imagined—intellectually, morally, or aesthetically.
Thus, as a person of Christian faith, I have sought to work out my
own intellectual, moral, and aesthetic positions within the bounds
of what I understand the best of the tradition to allow or even foster, but with the recognition that not all denominations or churches
will embrace or foster those things. I have struggled with the tradition and then seen if I can fit into the institution, and I have sought
to nudge the institution toward the best that it is capable of.

Although it was an intellectual search that was the first edge of
my relationship with Christianity, as I look at and listen to others I
know that questions of credibility, of truth, are not everyone's central religious questions. My second entrée into theological critique
came as a result of my discovery of feminism. Could there be a
Christianity that took seriously the growing number of struggles for
self-determination? As I recognized multiple entry points into
human questioning, I began to wonder whether there might be
ways to characterize religious searching that embraced my searches
for intellectual credibility and self-determination and yet were more
general than those searches.

What was it that I was searching for? My search for the intellectual credibility of Christianity and support for self-determination
was part of a broader search, not just for "meaning," but for what I
have come to think of as *flourishing*, which depends on what I will
here call *right relation* with the universe. This search is possible for
human beings because of their capacity for self-transcendence. I
am not seeking here to say this is every human being's search or
that everyone would articulate the search this way. What I will say
is that it seems to illumine my own situation and the situation in
which I find many of the people with whom I interact on a daily
basis. Although the terms sound generic, the reality of these
searches is profoundly contextual, for both flourishing and right
relationship can and do take a host of forms. If my characterization
sheds light on other very different human contextual realities, so
much the better.

Human beings engage in this search for what I am calling right
relation and flourishing in part because they can. It is a human
capacity to look beyond the immediate present and reflect on what has

proceeded it and on what might happen. Humans are continuously asking the question Why? because they can see that things do not have to be as they are.

But human beings also look for the possibilities of things being different from the way they are because there is lack of flourishing and right relation for so many. In the world today, there are many who have been treated as "nonpersons" whose capacity for freedom and self-determination has been severely curtailed by the contexts in which they live their lives.[3] Many, through no activity or lack of activity on their own, find themselves in situations where they do not have the material means to sustain life or where they have no political voice in the powers that keep their lives enslaved. Those who have been treated as nonpersons are voicing their protests and seeking a social and political world where all humanity can eat, live, and enjoy freedoms and self-determination.

The question Why? also extends to the plight of the earth. Many human beings have chosen to treat the nonhuman as that which is to be dominated and controlled, used and discarded, not valued in and for itself. Yet there are others who hear profound questions addressed to them by the rest of the world.[4] They are those for whom the situation of dominating and subduing the nonhuman raises profound questions about who we are as human beings in relation to what is not human. Many are beginning to search for another mode of relating that might recognize not only the damage that has been done to our nonhuman neighbors but also the distorted relationships that this has meant for humanity.

Material goods and self-determination are not the only things human beings search for. Those with plenty of material things can still experience something lacking in their lives. Today, the most common way to talk about the nonmaterial things for which human beings search is to name it a search for "spirituality." Such a search can be a search for explanation or for meaning: Why are things, ultimately, as they are, and how could they be different? What is it about the universe that makes it possible to look for flourishing existence? Such a search can also be a search for an existential sense of place and belonging. As Peter C. Emberley puts it in a recent issue of *MacLean's* magazine: "The reality is that many of them [baby boomers] are simply looking for a little grace and an opportunity to express indebtedness, fidelity and reverence."[5]

Self-transcendence

Karl Rahner characterizes the human search as one in which human beings are beings of transcendence beyond themselves to the one whom theists call God. According to Rahner, human searching takes three forms. The human being seeks justification for love and wants someone to love who deserves one's absolute love. Humans struggle with their own mortality and seek that which will afford them readiness for death. Human beings seek a future where there will be absolute reconciliation.[6] My own sense of the search is that Rahner has characterized well some of the problematics that are central to human struggling. The search for love, for meaning in the face of death, and for a different future has a dimension of ultimacy that forces one beyond the everyday to ask about oneself in light of the whole of which one is part.

The possibility of moving beyond ourselves is the possibility of self-transcendence. We can plan and dream beyond the here and now. We can see that the future could be different from the present. We can transcend our history by being able to envisage different possibilities, by recognizing that things could be different from how they are. This is not a utopian view of transcendence, in the sense of being "no place." The power of such transcendence lives from its possibility. The fact that we can envisage the possible that is not yet here allows us to build ideas of a different social and political world. Creativity depends on the ability to transcend the given, in thought and in action. Through self-transcendence we go beyond the traditional categories of philosophical and theological thought; we rethink old categories and invent new ones to suit present needs.

We can see and move beyond ourselves as individuals toward others, to the community, to the world, and to the whole, however it might be conceived. Through self-transcendence we can move beyond narrow self-interest to concern for what is beyond ourselves. In transcending the self we enter into relationships with others. To move beyond the self to relate to the other elicits the power that Audre Lorde calls the "erotic." Lorde says:

> The erotic functions for me in several ways, and the first is in providing the power that comes from sharing deeply any pursuit with another person. The sharing of joy, whether physical, emotional, psychic, or intellectual, forms a bridge between

the sharers that can be the basis for understanding much of what is not shared between them, and lessens the threat of their difference.[7]

The erotic allows the self to give and receive from another. It allows for values and dreams to be communally shared. Every time anyone discovers that her experiences are not isolated instances, but marks of a shared systemic and systematic oppression, she has experienced self-transcendence. The ability to experience oneself as part of something beyond oneself is a mark of self-transcendence.

Our possibility for self-transcendence also allows, perhaps forces, us to ask about our own limits and the possibilities of meaning given those limits. We reach beyond ourselves not only to the others with whom we interact to share the planet, but toward the whole and toward trying to conceive our own identities in relation to that whole. We know that we will die, and we know that our lives are full of the unpredictable and things that cannot be completely controlled. We reach toward the mystery of our life and lives in general, seeking to know how to relate to the whole.

Although self-transcendence allows us to move beyond the here and now, it does not necessarily need to draw us from concern for that here and now. Self-transcendence is a human possibility that allows for the search for flourishing and right relation that is so important to nonpersons today. Part of the challenge of those whose searching has traditionally been discounted is to keep the human possibility for self-transcendence from being used to draw concern away from our present realities to some truly utopian nonplace beyond rather than within history.

Flourishing

Flourishing is one broad way to characterize human seeking. To talk about flourishing is not to talk about one thing, but to talk about a multifaceted way to depict the fullness of human life that includes both material well-being and the possibility to expand one's intellectual and existential horizons. We do not have to use the same measures of flourishing for everyone. People can and ought to set their own standards for flourishing. That said, however, issues arise whenever the flourishing of some comes into conflict with the flourishing of others. And visions of possibilities for flourishing can be impeded by the fact that one's immediate possibilities seem so limited.

North American culture has become a culture of acquisition. Advertisers and multinational companies are constantly telling us that we will be happier if we have more things. Possibilities for flourishing can be impeded by having too many material things. One can take refuge in material things and define life and its possibilities totally in terms of acquisition. This is one situation where appeal to flourishing needs the further appeal to right relation (see below) to make clear that flourishing cannot simply be equated with having as many material things as possible. Acquiring and having lots of material things can get in the way of our asking ourselves questions about whether we are truly flourishing. But in the end, only some of our needs are material, and, especially if our having in overabundance is tied to others not having sufficient for existence, questions arise.

Beyond having our basic physical needs met, yet another aspect of providing possibilities for flourishing is some element of social/political determination. Not all of us would appear to desire or envision the same political and social systems. Yet, unless we can form and express opinions without fear of reprisals, our possibilities for self-actualization are seriously impeded. Flourishing also presupposes being treated by our social and political systems with a basic sense of fairness for all human beings. If such conditions are not given to all, then some flourish at the expense of others. Social-political determination takes places in communities. "Self-naming is a function incorporating the unique experience and perspective of individuals and groups within the wider community, but such naming widens the community yet further, and may even create an alternative community."[8]

To flourish is to exist as fully as possible, given that we never exist alone, but always in community with the others, human and non-human, with whom we share the planet. Flourishing, then, is about the whole of life, not about some small part of it, and about how all the parts relate to the whole, both of one's individual life and of one's life in world community.

We need intellectual challenge and stimulation. As those who can think beyond themselves, human beings are drawn into problem solving, not just for the sake of living, but for the sake of living better. We are drawn to think about pragmatic problems, the solutions to which will improve our material lives. We are also drawn to ponder questions of meaning and value, questions beyond the merely physical. We like to think for its own sake and to have something meaningful to think about. We seek opportunities for intellectual growth as well as material comfort. As creative beings, we seek outlets for our creativity. We design and enact; we explore the world around us and our own inner worlds.

We seek opportunities for other sorts of development, such as emotional growth. We seek to become fully mature individuals who know our selves well enough that we can name and find fulfillment for our emotional needs without compromising or harming ourselves or others. This means learning to trust our fully embodied selves as authorities on what we need. It means learning how to place in perspective the shame and guilt that we have internalized from our past and those who would control us.

We also seek growth in our explorations of self-transcendence. Flourishing is about joy, satisfaction, fulfillment. It is, in its broadest sense, aesthetic. To flourish is to live with a balance of harmony and intensity in one's life and in the life of the world.

> For each level of complexity there is a balance of unity and diversity which is ideally satisfying. What we spontaneously call beautiful exhibits this balance. Discord, diversity not integrated by unifying factors, is not very good; but too tame harmony or unity, not sufficiently diversified with contrasting aspects, is not very good either. And at the extreme limit, one form of aesthetic failure is as bad as the other; for in either case experience becomes impossible. To be bored to death is not better than to be shocked to death.[9]

I need to discern what enables me to live in harmony and contentment with the rest of the universe and it with me. Once we recognize the possibilities of self-transcendence toward another, called the "erotic" by Audre Lorde, we begin to understand what is possible for ourselves in terms of flourishing. "Once we begin to feel deeply all the aspects of our lives, we begin to demand from ourselves and from our life-pursuits that they feel in accordance with that joy which we know ourselves to be capable of."[10]

We do nothing as isolated individuals. We share a planet with many other beings. We enjoy the company of many others with whom we share the planet. Yet we also clash with others with whom we are sharing space and time. Even though we are not isolated individuals, some of us act as though only our flourishing counts, others' flourishing being easily sacrificed to our desires. To live oblivious to the flourishing of others is only possible for a small group of human beings. But other voices are beginning to assert themselves, challenging the flourishing of the few at the expense of the many, both human and nonhuman, whose well-beings intersect and interweave on this planet. Thus, the category of flourishing is not sufficient to understand human searching; we also need to explore what right relationship among existents might be if flourishing is to be for the many rather than for the few.

Much of what makes life worth living is in the relationships we have with others. We live in an interconnected web with others, human and nonhuman. Our lives are only possible because of our connections. So it is not a question of connection or not, but of what sort of connections we will have with others. Again the question of right relationship asserts itself.

Right Relation

How do I situate myself in relation to the whole of which I am a part in order to permit flourishing not just for myself but for the whole? Where do I stand in the universe? How should I understand my relationship to other human beings, to what is nonhuman, to the universe as a whole? Sometimes individual human beings or certain groups of human beings have acted as though they are the center of the universe, all else being expected to meet their particular needs. But such an approach to the world leaves out too much and allows for the triumph of the very few. It neglects most of humanity and all that is nonhuman, including whatever might be considered to be ultimate; that is, God. Those who have historically been considered nonpersons (among others: women, people of color, the disabled, gays and lesbians, those not from the northern hemisphere) are searching for an alternative to the dominance of the few and for possibilities for the flourishing of the many.

If the many are to flourish, then we need a sense of how those many might be rightly related to one another to allow that to happen, and we need to point to distortions of right relation that impede flourishing.

Relation is distorted when individuals or small groups of human beings take themselves to be the center or the whole of the universe. In right relation I understand myself as only one small part of a much greater whole. I understand that I am interconnected with others, not just human but nonhuman, and that my actions foster or impede their possibilities of flourishing. In right relation I view others not as instruments to my ends but as holding value for their own sakes. I am connected to others not in view of coercing them to my will, but through eros, which brings to us and others a sense of satisfaction and completion. "Once we know the extent to which we are capable of feeling that sense of satisfaction and completion, we can then observe which of our various life endeavors bring us closest to that fullness."[11]

Right relation is also about relating to myself. It is about valuing my whole self, my self as embodied being. It is about celebrating materiality alongside that which transcends the material. Self-transcendence may be necessary for flourishing, but so is valuing our embodied selves as good so that we value our connections to the concrete materiality in which it is ours to live. We are not disembodied self-transcenders. Self-transcendence requires materiality. For it is the material world in which we live and move and have our being that we can envisage as different and thus seek to change. It is the material world in which we must seek to live, for we have no other.

Right relation has both "metaphysical" and sociopolitical aspects. It is about how one stands in relation to the whole and about how one's life is constructed by self and others to allow for or to impede flourishing. Right relation is seeking to live with, not against, the universe. It is situating oneself in the universe vis-à-vis others.

These human searchings have a dimension of ultimacy about them. If life just provided these things, there would be no need to ponder them and no need for something like religion to suggest that things could and should be different from how they are. It is precisely because there are problems and questions that human beings have looked, among other places, to religious traditions to provide alternative views to draw us from our experienced lives into the possibilities of something different.

The dimension of ultimacy in human questions has been one of the things that religious traditions, including Christianity, have sought to attend to; that is, to take the actual, the world as it is, and relate it to the possibilities, both positive and negative, for human thought and action in the world. In such ways as through symbols, narratives, and rituals, religious traditions have sought to bring the actual and the possible into focus for their adherents. Religious traditions have sought to help people struggle with the question of what it means to be human and how, as human, to live rightly and well in the universe. This said, however, religious traditions are also products of their own times, places, and histories. Although they seek to provide humans with ways to situate themselves in the universe, they themselves have often become mired in the social and political thoughts and structures of their own times. Thus, in the present, far from being the source of anything like human flourishing, many religious traditions have found themselves implicated in impeding flourishing by fostering a status quo, both in their own institutional forms and in the societies in which their adherents live.

Because all religious questions find their life only in particular contexts, this book will look at one specific set of examples—that of Christian churches at the turn of the millennium. Can churches—with their mixture of the ideal and the historical-institutional as we inherit it in this time and, primarily, in this North American context—speak to human searching as I have outlined it in this chapter? Can Christian churches today speak to the human search for right relation and flourishing? What resources do they have to draw on that may allow them to speak to this search? In what ways have they impeded, even negated, this search?

Challenges to Christian Churches

Can Christianity, as a religious tradition with the church as its institutional form, foster flourishing and right relationship at the turn of the millennium? The question itself implies at least two assumptions. First, it assumes that it is at least part of the business of Christianity to foster the meeting of these human needs. Second, it assumes that there are some problems in its doing so at this time.

As a religious tradition with a long history, Christianity already has religious symbols, traditions, rituals, institutional forms, and so on, that are treated by some within the tradition as unalterable givens. But anyone with historical consciousness can observe that

Christianity has changed over time and that Christianity in the present is not one monolithic tradition but many variations of tradition living under the same name. Christian believers need to sort out what is central to the tradition and what is peripheral; what can and does change with the historical time and geographical location and what cannot be compromised. It is precisely the task of Christian theology to present an understanding of the Christian faith for its own time and place. If Christianity were able to be stated once and for all, or if the church took only one form, there would be no need for ongoing searching for ways to articulate and live the Christian faith in a variety of contexts.

If Christianity loses sight of what human beings are searching for, it becomes not a living religion but a dead one. Unless churches help people struggle with questions that people really are asking, churches become irrelevant to peoples' lives. This does not mean that people are not true to a tradition's roots and its central claims. But unless these claims tell the truth about human existence and tell it in a way that contemporary human beings can understand, appropriate, and live, then the claims are useless. In my Canadian context today, the churches as the institutional forms of Christianity are challenged, not so much through people directly asking questions, but through people not bothering to affiliate. In the once-mainline churches, which in Canada means such churches as The United Church of Canada, the Presbyterian Church in Canada, the Evangelical Lutheran Church in Canada, the Anglican Church of Canada, and the Roman Catholic Church, attendance is on a downward spiral.[12] I do know that in some areas of the United States church attendance is still high and that in Canada some evangelical churches are growing. But this does not take away from the challenges that I am going to name. These challenges arise in the North American context from those who question societal institutions with a view to asking how the institution benefits from maintaining alliances with the powerful and privileged in society. These people do not want to be part of anything that will not support them as individuals and the causes they hold important such as the environment or justice concerns. They are people who ask questions about what seems to them to be unsupported argument and uninterrogated tradition. They want to make their own moral decisions and do not want to function under the sway of what they see as the unfounded guilt and shame that seem to them to infect their parents or earlier generations. They know there are many ways to think or act and that choices must be made.

Most of the undergraduate students who come into my classes in religious studies have a firm idea that Christianity is a religious tradition that has univocal, set answers to unambiguous, set questions and that, to be part of Christianity, one must accept both the questions and the answers as given. In short, one of the challenges facing Christianity today is that many perceive it as dogmatic, offering pat (and outdated) answers to questions no one is really asking. For these students, and, I suspect, for many others, the church is not living and relevant to the issues they face daily. They think that there is only one way to view and speak of the Christian God—as white, male, and wielding coercive power. They think that if they are struggling with whether life has meaning, Christianity will not help with that struggle because it will give them only one pre-packaged answer to the struggle. They think that all churches oppose birth control or freedom of choice on the matter of unwanted pregnancy because they hear in the media only the official position of the Roman Catholic Church on such matters. This challenge, as I see it, is the challenge of whether the churches as the institutionalized forms of Christianity are willing to appear and portray themselves less as confidently providing answers and more as places to engage in the process of helping people in their own quests of dealing with the Ultimate. Of course Christianity has made and continues to make affirmations about God, ourselves, and the world in which we live, some of which I, for one, would not want to compromise. But question and compromise are two very different things. The challenge to Christian churches is not only to be, but also to appear to be, open to the religious questions that people have. Churches themselves have often made claims about holding fast and being unchanging against the winds of contemporary issues. Churches need to own how they have changed over time rather than portraying and presuming themselves as unchanging and unchangeable. One of the challenges churches face is how to change with the times so that they can meet human need without losing a sense of mission and identity and without compromising what they take to be central to the gospel. The challenge is the challenge of discerning when to change and when to stand firm.

Another challenge facing churches is their historic linkages with the powers of the status quo. These linkages have allied the church with the powerful, which has resulted in churches' complicity in a variety of oppressive forms as it takes on the lineaments of the powerful in society: for example, with racism, with sexism, with imperialism.

Since Constantine, the church in the West has been linked with the rulers of Empire. The interests of mission and the interests of expansion of territory have often been linked.[13] Working from its understanding of an imperative to convert the world to Christianity, the church has exported not only the gospel, but Western ways. At its worst it has condoned cultural and even actual genocide in the name of salvation. In North America, the churches have benefited from links with power by gaining recognition in society among the privileged and protected institutions. Clergy and leaders have often enjoyed being consulted by governments or recognized as important. Churches have had great freedoms. But this unrestricted freedom has not necessarily meant that the churches have been engaged as much as they might in criticizing systemic forces that might be seen as antithetical to the gospel. If one enjoys the status that comes with power, one might be reluctant to give it up by criticizing the powers that confer the status.

In their conviction that they possess the only access to God, salvation, and religious truth, Christian churches have often sought to eliminate all religious competitors without listening to what they have to say about what is ultimate for them. Perhaps the most extreme forms of this move came in the Crusades and in the witch-hunts, but until the mid–twentieth century most churches had policies of missionizing that called for the conversion of the whole world to Christianity. Today, however, more and more people are refusing to accept that there is only one religious way to see the world. Insofar as they reject this view, they reject Christian exclusivism, which is popularly seen to be the only Christian view. The average North American Christian now knows practitioners of other religious traditions and knows these people to be as faithful and moral as anyone in the churches. The churches need to struggle with presenting and understanding the Christian tradition in ways that do not demand the denigrating of other ways of being religious.[14]

In Western society, those who have been dominant have traditionally been white, male, heterosexual, and middle- to upper-class. Those who fit this profile have also traditionally been in positions of power in the mainline Christian churches. The most publicly visible forms of the Christian church are also the most hierarchical. In particular, because it has a single worldwide organization rather than varying national forms of organization, the Roman Catholic Church, with its hierarchy, has been highly visible. Churches, especially those who are trying to get away from at least the most overt forms of the traditional hierarchies, face the challenge that outsiders do not know that church leadership is shared more widely than by a group of celibate, mostly white, males. Many North Americans today expect to have some share in the decision making of the organizations to which they belong.

Since the mid–twentieth century, challenges have been voiced to Christianity by "nonpersons," those who have not been part of the traditional Christian elite.[15] Women have begun to articulate how the Christian church, both in its theology and in its actions, has been complicitous in maintaining patriarchy, both within itself and within society. They have begun to question the portrayal of God as unrelentingly male. They have refused to belong to churches that will not accept their leadership. They have rejected texts that seem to allow only patriarchal interpretations. Persons of color have noted Christian complicity in racism, sometimes actively through continued segregation of churches, sometimes passively through refusing to challenge deeply held ways of thinking about who is really in the image of God and who is not. Lesbians and gays are barred from active leadership in many parts of the Christian church and are treated with contempt as the lowest of the low by churches that refuse to deal directly and honestly with their own fears of sexuality. Those from the lower classes have begun to challenge a church that does not itself challenge the economic status quo that keeps them poor.

Many "nonpersons" in society have dismissed the church entirely as irrelevant to their lives, or they are challenging churches to show how they can promote flourishing and right relation not just for the elite, but for all humankind.

Since 1967, when Lynn White wrote his now-famous essay "The Historic Roots of Our Ecologic Crisis," Christianity has also been seen as, at best, complicitous with, at worst, cause of, our current ecological crises.[16] Christianity has been perceived as anthropocentric, seeing humanity as the pinnacle of creation and concerned only with human well-being, ignoring the well-being of the rest of creation. Interpreting the Genesis story to mean that humans should have the absolute right to manipulate the rest of creation for human ends, the Christian churches have often supported a hierarchical worldview that places humans and God together on the higher side of a great divide that has everything else in creation on its other side. Then, identifying humans with God, we have taken prerogative to do what we please with the rest of creation, often to its peril as though we were not ourselves part of creation.

The challenges from women, from lesbians and gays, from the ecologically aware, and from others combine also in a challenge of the church's fear of body, embodiment, and all the goods of the body, including sexual expression, which is often expressed theologically as an exaltation of disembodied spirit and a subordination of material life in the world. So the church is seen as fearful of sexuality and, because fearful, seeking to control sexuality with taboos and rules.[17] Rather than discuss sexuality as part of God's good creation, churches have often refused discussion of the goodness of sexuality or the pleasure of sexual relationship. Instead of discussing the quality and commitment of a relationship of which sexuality might be part, some churches have made pronouncements that restrict sex to heterosexual marriage and emphasize the possibility of procreation, rather than understanding sexuality as part of a continuum of intimacy and relationship. Such restrictions both diminish sexuality as good and do not take seriously the reality of people's lives as lived in North America today. When these views are seen as the view of "the church," churches appear to many as totally anachronistic on the matter of sex. This fear of embodiment can also be seen as encouraging a lack of commitment to social and ecological change, pointing us instead to a better, future, otherworldly life. If bodies are not important or valued for themselves, then why bother with trying to change physical circumstances here and now?

Christian claims and symbols are often couched in the language of ages past, and they draw on concepts that do not speak to contemporary human beings. We do not talk of "natures," "persons," and "substances" in the same way today as was done in the fourth and fifth centuries of this era, making our traditional ways of talking of Jesus Christ or the Trinity seem obscure to many. Our language can serve to exclude those who are not already insiders. This holds for using the philosophical language of another era. It also holds in terms of the conceptual language and images that communicate messages beyond what we take ourselves to be saying. I am thinking of the common use of only male language for God, even

though we profess that we all know that God is not biologically
male; or the portrayal of Jesus as blond and blue-eyed, even when
we know he was a Middle Eastern Jew. The challenge facing
Christianity is to speak to the present in language and concepts that
make sense in the present to those who are not necessarily conver-
sant with the historical tradition.

But it is not only that the language is incomprehensible. The
concepts and symbols have to be credible in terms of speaking to
the challengers. There are, for example, many ways to talk about
the power of God or the activity of God in the world.[18] Christians
need to seek ways that are credible to those whose view of the world
includes contemporary science and historical consciousness.
People who are convinced of the freedom and importance of their
choices to what happens in the world will not accept a view of God
that portrays God as a coercive despot whose world is one where
everything that happens depends on God and not on human
choice. People who are seeking to change social systems to benefit
the many rather than a privileged few, and who understand the
human construction of such structures, will not accept a view of
God that says that God creates the structures of society as God
wants them to be. Not all views of God are equal or equally credible in the contemporary world.

Many of those who are voicing the challenges mentioned above
see "the Christian church" as monolithic, one entity, with one
point of view, unchangeable over all time. That this view often lacks
nuance, however, is not a reason to dismiss the challenges. Indeed,
it would seem that the Christian church, in its various branches,
has a public relations nightmare on its hands. For every one of these
challenges one can find ample exemplary material to support argu-
ments that the Christian church impedes flourishing and right relation. In this book I sometimes talk of "the church" not because I
think of it as one entity, but because that is often the way it is experienced by outsiders. Those of us who are part of the church know
that there is great variety from denomination to denomination and
from congregation to congregation in terms of organization, theology, and practice. Some Christian churches, both denominations
and congregations, are seriously seeking to understand and meet
the challenges of the sort I describe here. Part of that challenge is
to break down the popular view of the church as having a single
structure and point of view. One of the challenges is publicity. How

can a church (denomination or local congregation) that tries to meet these challenges let the world know what it is doing?

Another challenge for the churches is that traditional patterns of belonging are changing. People no longer belong to traditional communities that are given to them by history. Although the debate about whether "community" is dying or just being reconstructed in multiple ways is an open one, what this has meant for churches is that belonging to churches simply because of past tradition cannot be taken for granted. People now choose whether or not to belong.[19]

The church is being challenged both in terms of its theological stances and in terms of its institutional organization and activity. Those of us inside the church know that not all challenges apply equally to all branches of the Christian church, nor to all individual congregations or believers. But the challenges themselves are real and important. If the churches cannot provide what people are seeking, they are irrelevant. Yet the church also needs to be wary of selling out to the winds of popular opinion simply to protect itself from extinction. If the church is to change, it needs to change in ways faithful to its gospel message, ways that benefit all of humanity and all of creation, not just a few.

We are living in a post-Christian world. We can no longer assume that Christianity will go unchallenged, either in its institutions or its theology. Nor can we assume that religious searches will see Christianity as the obvious choice. Nor can we count on cultural dominance to provide churches with full pews. We cannot easily trot out the answer "secularism" to the question of why people are not flocking to the church. It is not that people are not searching. They are not looking, however, to the kind of institution that many perceive the church to be.

At times, as someone who recognizes the challenges as legitimate and yet who remains within the Christian church, I feel like something of an anachronism. It has taken a lot of hard work to stay, a lot of searching beyond the surface, of reformation and revision. Yet stay I do. I do not by any means think that everyone can or ought to have her or his needs met by the Christian message. There are times when, despite my commitment to what I take to be the central message of the gospel, I am frustrated by the institutions who seek to articulate and communicate that gospel. Yet I meet people who are searching for the flourishing and right relation that I think Christianity has the resources to provide.

It is precisely to the matter of the resources available to Christianity to meet the challenges I have outlined that the rest of this project will turn. What resources can Christianity draw on if it seeks to speak to the human needs for right relation and flourishing? What would a church who sought to meet these challenges look like? How would it act?

NOTES

1. For a discussion of the problems with essentialism in the context of Religious Studies, see Mary Gerhart, "Framing Discourse for the Future," in Morny Joy and Eva Neumaier-Dargyay, eds., *Gender, Genre and Religion: Feminist Reflections* (Waterloo, Ont.: Wilfrid Laurier University Press, 1995), 22–27.

2. William P. Alston, "Religion," in *The Encyclopedia of Philosophy* 7:141–42.

3. Any number of groups could be mentioned: for example, aboriginal persons in North America or Australia, Tibetans, African Americans, women.

4. There are many recent books on religion and ecology. See, for example, David E. Cooper and Joy A. Palmer, eds., *Spirit of the Environment: Religion, Value and Environmental Concern* (New York: Routledge, 1998); Roger S. Gottlieb, ed., *This Sacred Earth: Religion, Nature, Environment* (New York: Routledge, 1996); Mary Ellen Tucker and John A. Grimm, eds., *Worldviews and Ecology: Religion, Philosophy and the Environment* (Maryknoll: Orbis Books, 1994).

5. Peter C. Emberley, "Searching for Purpose," *MacLean's*, December 28, 1998/January 4, 1999.

6. See, for example, Karl Rahner, "Jesus Christ: History of Dogma and Theology," in Karl Rahner, ed., *Encyclopedia of Theology: The Concise Sacramentum Mundi* (New York: Seabury, 1975), 753–55.

7. Audre Lorde, "Uses of the Erotic: The Erotic as Power," in Judith Plaskow and Carol Christ, eds., *Weaving the Visions: New*

Patterns in Feminist Spirituality (San Francisco: Harper & Row, 1989), 210.

8. Marjorie Hewitt Suchocki, "The Search for Justice: Religious Pluralism from a Feminist Perspective," in John Hick and Paul Knitter, eds., *The Myth of Christian Uniqueness: Toward a Pluralistic Theology of Religions* (Maryknoll: Orbis Books, 1987), 155.

9. Charles Hartshorne, *Creative Synthesis and Philosophic Method* (LaSalle, Ill.: Open Court, 1970), 304.

10. Lorde, "Uses of the Erotic," 211.

11. Ibid., 209.

12. See Reginald W. Bibby, *Unknown Gods: The Ongoing Story of Religion in Canada* (Toronto: Stoddard, 1993), 3–11.

13. See, for example, Douglas John Hall, *The Future of the Church: Where Are We Headed?* (Toronto: The United Church Publishing House, 1989), 23ff.

14. See, for example, Pamela Dickey Young, *Christ in a Post-Christian World: How Can We Believe in Jesus Christ When Those Around Us Believe Differently—or Not at all?* (Minneapolis: Fortress, 1995).

15. See, for example, Claude Geffré, "A Prophetic Theology," in Alfred T. Hennelly, ed., *Liberation Theology: A Documentary History* (Maryknoll: Orbis Books, 1990), 182.

16. Lynn White, Jr., "The Historic Roots of our Ecologic Crisis," in David and Eileen Spring, eds., *Ecology and Religion in History* (New York: Harper & Row, 1974), 15–31.

17. For discussions of Christianity and sexuality, see, for example, Lisa Sowle Cahill, *Between the Sexes: Foundations for a Christian Ethics of Sexuality* (Philadelphia: Fortress, 1985); Beverly Wildung Harrison and Carter Heyward, "Pain and Pleasure: Avoiding the Confusions of Christian Tradition in Feminist Theory," in James B. Nelson and Sandra P. Longfellow, eds., *Sexuality and the Sacred: Sources for Theological Reflection* (Louisville: Westminster/John Knox, 1994),131–48; L. J. Tessier, *Dancing After the Whirlwind: Feminist Reflections on Sex, Denial, and Spiritual Transformation* (Boston: Beacon, 1997), 57–63.

18. Anna Case-Winters, *God's Power: Traditional Understandings and Contemporary Challenges* (Louisville: Westminster/John Knox, 1990).

19. For an intelligent discussion of this debate, see Nancy Tatom Ammerman, with Arthur E. Farnsley II et al., *Congregation and Community* (New Brunswick: Rutgers University Press, 1997), 349–55.

2. Churches as Communities of Eros

I look to Christianity as one possibility for fostering flourishing and right relationship, not because I think Christianity, or its institutional forms in the Christian churches, is the only or even the most likely place to encounter such fostering. Indeed, the challenges from the last chapter might make a reader wonder if one should bother with the church at all. Yet, for reasons that are born both of my own experience in the church and of my theological thinking about what the church could and should be, I think there are resources that churches are not fully using that, if developed, could be a force in the flourishing and right relationship that many people are seeking. From another perspective, I think that if the church is to survive as a meaningful institution rather than as a sociopolitical anachronism into the twenty-first century, churches must begin or continue to attend to some of the challenges that have been mentioned.

The church is not monolithic. The church is made up of very diverse denominations that vary not only because of denominational history but also because of their contextual situations in time and place. In addition, within denominations there are many varied individual churches who take part of their identity from their denominational background but who exist in their own, sometimes stunning, individuality. This individuality may be fostered or hampered by various denominational structures and authorities. Here, even though I sometimes talk about the church in the singular, the variability of individual denominations and congregations means that the actual embodiment of Christianity is plural—in churches.

My own vision of church is born of several sources. The view that I present is consonant with the biblical sources, which, as I argue below, do not posit a single definition or authority structure for the church. It is compatible with and, indeed, advances the gospel message as I understand it. The definition seeks to be broad rather than narrow, thus encompassing as widely as possible various instantiations of church in the contemporary world. That said, it clearly grows out of the Protestant tradition, although I hope that it is also recognizable and appealing to some Roman Catholics. It does not recognize or privilege the locus of church in an apostolic succession of the ordained hierarchy. I present this vision as one that might meet contemporary needs as those were articulated earlier in this book. I know that individual denominations and congregations will not all be equally willing first, to agree with the vision, and second, to try to see themselves and act in accord with it.

It is my conviction that as a definition, and therefore as an ideal, the working definition of church that I present here is one that could serve the churches well if they are truly seeking to be church and to meet religious needs at the turn of the millennium.

What should Christian churches seek to be at the turn of the millennium? How can they understand and present themselves to others? I propose a vision of church as *a diverse collection of communities of eros finding their common identity in the shared memory and presence of Jesus Christ and seeking to embody God's transforming grace by fostering flourishing and right relationship for all creation.*

In the next chapters of this book I will unpack this definition bit by bit. As a whole, it is meant to function as an ideal, as a guide to churches seeking to be what they are called to be. Because the definition is an ideal, individual denominational and congregational lives may not totally embody that ideal. It is also true that denominations and congregations have many more facets than can be included in one definition.

An ideal definition needs concrete embodiment if it is to mean anything at all. I think that churches, both denominations and congregations, could come closer to the ideal than most do. If they do not, churches risk even more being seen as irrelevant. It is my own conviction that the church has potential. Perhaps this is a pretentious thing to say in the context of an institution that has often enjoyed, and in many ways still enjoys, all the trappings of being associated with power and privilege. What I mean is that churches have resources in the gospel and in their ways of being that can, if they are only used, allow churches to speak to those who are religious seekers today in a way that does not give definitive answers, but rather enters the religious struggle alongside these seekers.

Eros

The church is a diverse collection of communities of eros. To those who have been taught the traditional ways of speaking of love, this at first sounds odd. We have been taught that eros, erotic love, is not so much a good as a necessary evil, bound up with sexuality and properly used for procreation. In the history of the Christian tradition, the dominant way to speak of love has been as *agape*. The love that Christians have been taught and invited to enact as agape has been characterized as self-sacrificing, self-giving, never seeking anything in return. It has been said to mirror the love of God for us and the love that the earthly Jesus expressed.

Admittedly, the New Testament does not use the Greek word *eros* when it talks about love. I use it here as an English word, however, because I think it better captures for us at the turn of the millennium the spirit of the love attested in the biblical witness. We often read the New Testament use of agape through the lens of self-effacement and self-sacrifice, of giving without the connection of receiving. Although agape is the biblical term that is most often used to indicate "love," it is a theological decision, rather than one in line with biblical usage, to see this love in only one way.[1] The New Testament use of agape encompasses a whole range of loving, not just self-sacrificial love.[2] I could simply use the term *love* without a gloss, but I choose to use eros to explicate this love as a way to draw our attention to elements of love that have traditionally been neglected in theological discussion.

There are several reasons why I think it no longer suffices to talk of Christian love as a disinterested and self-sacrificing love. Here I mean to include all loving relationships: the love of God for us, our love for God, the love of God experienced through Jesus the Christ, and the love we ought to have for one another. Such a concept of love makes more sense, perhaps, when the idea of God with which one is working is the unmoved mover inherited from Greek thought. If stasis is perfection, then a one-sided love that gives but never receives is understandable. But most Christian attempts to conceive of God, including the ways in which God is portrayed in the biblical witness, go far beyond the notion of static perfection even if, when pushed to speak of God in strictly definitional terms, many might still resort to the notion of unchangeability. The biblical God is not the disinterested God of the Greeks, the one whose perfections cannot be added to or subtracted from. The God of the Bible is one who offers relationship and who is overjoyed when a lost sheep returns to the fold or a lost coin is found. God is one who suffers what the world suffers. God rejoices when creatures make choices that foster flourishing and right relationship. In the New Testament, God's love is precisely passionate love for creation and for humanity within it. The appropriate response is one of "passion for God, the passion of a little flock which perseveres faithfully and unshakeably" in God's love.[3] God is a God of eros.

Christians talk about their experiences of God as if they make a difference to God. When we address God in prayer or reflect with others about our relationship with God, we do it in terms that suggest that God cares passionately about us as individuals and that what we do affects God, for better or for worse. We think of ourselves as interacting with God, not just reacting to God.

Interaction requires a relationship where God responds. Therefore, God changes in response to what I do so that the interaction and the relationship is real, based on my very specificity and particularity. In my view, a God who is worthy of worship is profoundly relational. That relationship is a relationship of mutuality, or mutual enrichment, of give and take. Such a relationality is what I am here calling eros.[4] God is enriched by the values we create, whether it be the value of truth when we discover metaphysics or science; the value of moral goodness, creating justice; the value of beauty by enriching ourselves, others, and God. Conversely, God is not enriched when our choices cause suffering to others in the world and, indeed, to God.

The God I am portraying here is not a fickle God, one who changes on a whim or whose reaction is as ephemeral as a breeze. God's love is steadfast and everlasting for every individual in the universe, but that steadfast and everlasting love takes concrete form in relation to individuals and specific situations.[5]

As I will argue in more detail below, the focal point of Christology is itself relational. Jesus' relationship to his followers is not one of disinterest. What his followers do in response is of profound importance to Jesus. In the gospel stories Jesus loves and is loved in return.

In the Christian tradition we have shied away from eros for several reasons. We have feared that any assertion of need or of the potential goodness of receiving as well as giving might plunge us into an egotism that asserts the self above all others. We have read Jesus' injunctions to love our enemies, do good to those who hate us, turn the other cheek, and give what is needed, including the clothes off our backs (Luke 6:27–30) as calls to selflessness. In the dominant trajectory of Christianity, we have been profoundly afraid of the self, as if even admitting a self would lead us into immediate selfishness and egocentricity. But not all love that is mutually enriching is by definition merely egotistical or self-serving, and not all love that regards the other and the other's needs with utmost seriousness requires us to evacuate the self. Indeed, the Lukan passage paraphrased above ends with the phrase "Do to others as you would have them do to you" (Luke 6:31). Thus the admonition here is not to give away the self, but to regard the other as the self.

We have feared our bodies and, of most importance, our sexuality. Because eros has been so closely associated with sexuality and sexual desire, rather than grapple with the ways in which desire might be a positive as well as a negative value, we have stepped back from the erotic altogether without taking its religious potential seriously enough.

Eros as I mean the term is not the same as lust. The connection between eros and lust is desire, but that which separates these two is the mutuality of relationship that accompanies true eros. Eros encompasses sexual love, but it is much more. It is the passionate feeling that connects us to one another and to the whole. "[T]his deep, wild, embodied power has an even greater reach; it is, in fact, the very heart of our desire, our awareness of and longing for interconnectedness with all things."[6] Desire is the desire for the other, the desire to know, to understand, to be in intimate relationship with another. It is profoundly interested in the other. Interest does not need to be merely self-serving. In eros I am not interested in the other as servant of my interests. Whereas in lust, whether the lust for sex or power or money, others become mere objects, instruments of my grasping, in true eros my desire meets the interests of the other, indeed of many others, in a way that enriches both me and the ones with whom I am in relation. What happens to the other makes a difference, a profound difference, for in a relationship of mutuality, I am moved by the other. What the other enjoys brings enjoyment to me, and what the other suffers brings suffering.

In eros I make a commitment to those to whom I relate. I say, "You matter to me. Our fates are inextricably intertwined." I love the other as myself.

Creativity is animated by eros, as is knowledge. As heirs of Enlightenment tradition, many of us have been taught to value "objectivity," to think that the more we can remove ourselves from the "object" of our focus, the more truly we will "know" it. But both the value and the possibility of such a separation have come into question in recent decades. The possibility of such a separation has been questioned by those of traditionally nondominant groups (e.g., women, persons of color) who have noted that supposedly objective knowledge often serves to privilege those in power and ignore or caricature those in the nondominant groups. For example, the growth of male-controlled objective medical knowledge led to experimental control groups of men, with conclusions about women simply being generalized from the data about men. There has been a lack of data specifically about women, yet we are beginning to realize that women's bodies may react differently from men's to disease and treatment. As many scholars have begun to ask whether there is any objective knowledge, they have also begun to question why such supposed objective knowledge has been taken as a privileged form of knowledge. As humans we do not choose that which we study or relate to out of disinterest. A scholar is drawn to the subject matter that she studies. She is profoundly interested in the subject and the outcome or she would not invest all the time and energy she does in understanding. Likewise, the artist is animated by commitment to the materials he uses in the creative process and by the vision of the outcome. Eros is not about the knowledge that controls, that "masters" its object, but about knowledge that interacts with the subject of its interests, that is changed by that subject. Although one might think that scientific knowledge is different from the sort of interaction I portray here, such scientists as Nobel Prize winner Barbara McClintock testified to an intimate personal relationship with the corn plants she studied.

By confusing eros with lust we have contributed to the denigration of both sexuality and embodiment in Christian tradition. If love is not at all interested in the self, then we do not have to pay serious attention to the embodied self and its needs and desires. Our way of dealing with fears about our own desires has often been to pretend they do not exist. We pretend to ignore our own bodies, even though the admonitions of the gospel to love the neighbor are often admonitions to take care precisely of the bodily needs of another. Our pitting of agape against eros is a way to ignore rather than deal seriously and directly with our sexual urges. But if we take the physical needs of others seriously, this means reclaiming the goodness of embodiment and seeking to deal with it in all its goodness while at the same time recognizing and combating the distortions of love to which all embodiment might tempt us.

Eros is not just a relationship of one person to one other person. The erotic is a component of all of our relationships including our relationships to what is not human, our relationships to groups as well as to individuals, and our relationship to God. "At the most fundamental level, the erotic connects us to the sacred. This is nothing new. Prayer and ritual, art and music, even our most intense emotional relationships, emphasize this connection."[7]

One can be deeply committed to the life of a group as well as to the life of a single other. The disinterested and self-sacrificing love that is often called agape will not suffice as the glue to hold the community of the church together. Passionate commitment to the life of the church is necessary for the church to live the gospel in the world. Such passionate commitment means that one is changed in the process.

One problem with the notion of the church as a community of self-sacrifice is that it loses sight of the value of the individuals who make it up. Passionate commitment does not mean seeking only one's own good. The true relationality of eros is not egocentric to the exclusion of the other, but wills the good of self and other together. This does not mean that there will not be conflicts that might arise when the good of the self differs from the good of the other, whether a single other or a communal other. What it does mean, however, is that it is not eros in and of itself that is the problem.

This point might be well illustrated by returning to the traditional notion of agape. One of the reasons that the Christian tradition has concentrated so much on the self-sacrificing ideal of agape has been, I think, a matter of conviction that the distortions of eros can run rampant, whereas agape cannot be distorted. It is only recently that feminist theology has begun to point to the distortions of agape.[8] The distortions of agape are such things as lack of focus, lack of an organizing center, lack of a self, and such distortions have historically been far more prevalent in women than in men in the Western world.

In the Western world where individualism seems to have triumphed, where individual interests usually dominate the interests of groups or of the whole, the connectedness of eros seems far more needed than the detachment of agape.

I speak of churches as communities of eros to emphasize the importance of connection, of commitment, of relationality within the church, as well as to point to the needed commitment of churches to the world beyond their boundaries.

Communities

By portraying churches as communities of eros, I mean to highlight the connectedness and connection that is essential to eros while at the same time pointing to the intentionality of these particular gatherings rather than the random connections that we make throughout our lives. Churches are not a hodgepodge of isolated individuals, but coherent groups with a reason and a focus for their existence as groups.

North Americans at this point in their history are highly individualistic. Especially in the United States, and to a lesser extent in Canada, we are more prone to assert the rights and privileges of individuals rather than those of groups. Such a move is not accidental. It serves to protect the privilege of the traditionally powerful and wealthy by refusing to recognize that they too are often members of a group, the group of the mostly white, mostly male, upper class.

Indeed, most of the liberation movements of the twentieth century have been based on a notion of communal identity, of something shared by virtue of which access to the goods of society have been denied (ethnicity or sex, for example). Naysayers to such liberation movements have often criticized such movements precisely on the basis of individualism without recognizing that they gain their privilege in large part by belonging to those for whom the "playing field" has been heavily weighted in favor of success. For example, the entry of women into professions such as medicine, law, or ministry has tended to obscure the fact that they are still often treated as exceptions to the norm. If we have passed the era of doctors and "lady doctors," ministers and "lady ministers," we are not far past it.

But even if we tend first to individualism in our society, we cannot deny that human existence is irreducibly social. Although we often mask them or pretend we do not need them, we cannot exist without social connections that we may recognize only by their absence. If garbage collectors withdraw their labor in a big city, people notice. If mothers withdraw their labor in a family, people notice. The more complex the society, the more we depend on others, but the more removed we are from those others as human beings. The question is not whether to be connected to others, but how. With what measure of mindfulness and care will we make and sustain our connections? We can go through our days without any awareness of the others around us except as servants of our needs. The woman behind the counter in the coffee shop is not really a woman, but a coffee-pouring machine. The mechanic in the garage is an extension of the tools needed to fix the car. When we regard those others to whom we are connected as objects or instruments to further our own individual purposes, we refuse to see them as those with whom we should be in an I-Thou relationship.[9] We see ourselves, not in communities, but as isolated individuals trying to "get ahead."

Some people call themselves Christians but refuse to affiliate with the organized church in any way. There are undoubtedly a variety of reasons for this. For some it is a matter of individualism. They see Christianity as a set of beliefs and/or moral practices that can be adhered to without any formal connection to others who hold those same beliefs or share those moral practices. For these people, salvation is usually understood as a transaction between them and Jesus/God rather than as that which might be sought in community with others.

For some, church as organized community has been a place where they have not experienced the fullness of life that they believe is central to the Christian message. They see the message contradicted by the community seeking to transmit that message, and so they seek to live what they understand to be the Christian message apart from a community existence within an institutional church. They may seek community elsewhere with those with whom they share values or other commitments, but they do not look to a church to provide a community of belonging, a community of which they can feel part, one that nourishes their commitment to living out the gospel.

But even those who think of themselves as Christian yet do not formally affiliate themselves with the church as an institution depend on this same church for the transmission of Christian tradition. Unless the Christian tradition had been handed on through those who call themselves Christians, the tradition itself would not be a living option. Even if we are critical of some of the ways in which churches have passed on the tradition or have acted in the passing on of that tradition, the tradition itself survives largely because communities called churches have kept it alive. One can read the texts of any religious tradition and perhaps find them moving and edifying. But the richness of a tradition survives well beyond its texts in the lives of those for whom it has had central meaning.

Nor did Christianity begin as a tradition of the book. Early Christians did, of course, have the texts of Judaism. But long before the texts of Christianity, there were groups of followers of Jesus who shared their stories and their lives. The beginnings of Christianity were communal, and the church as an institution developed out of the loosely formed community of those who responded to Jesus directly or to the recounting of Jesus' effect on others.

We form ourselves into communities for a variety of purposes: economic, social, educational, recreational, reproductive, just to name a few examples. Some communities, like the nuclear family, are seen as normative in North American society. Even though most of us do not actually belong to a family grouping in the normative expectation of two parents plus children, the expectation itself is seen as the norm. In some parts of North America, belonging to the Christian church is also seen as normative, even though North America is religiously diverse and pluralistic.

In rural areas in Canada, for instance, the normativity of the Christian church often prevails even when the congregation is growing older and is not replaced by the young of the villages who do not often attend church. In certain areas of the United States, churches are growing rather than shrinking, giving the impression that we do not have to grapple with religious diversity. People in some communities, both large and small, are "expected" to belong to a Christian church.

But for most of us in North America at the turn of the millennium, affiliation with a church community is a personal option rather than a normative expectation. We know that both our systems of belief and our communities of affiliation are self-chosen rather than given by God or the fates. We know that these same beliefs and communities, however we may relate them in the long run to divine revelation, are humanly constructed and can be humanly changed. Holding Christian faith or belonging to a church are choices that people make from a vast variety of possible ways in which one might choose to live one's life.

Thus the communities of eros that are churches are voluntary communities. Today in North America people can opt in and out with very few consequences. This situation does, of course, vary from place to place, but it is vastly different from a time when one had to subscribe to the thirty-nine Articles of the Church of England in order to attend Oxford University, or when one risked being burned as a witch if one's beliefs or life were not thought orthodox. We have become increasingly aware of the voluntary nature of religious belief. We recognize, in view of the fact that everyday we meet others who have made other religious choices, that we need more and more to own whatever religious faith we might have rather than to adopt the stances of our ancestors.

Churches are active choices rather than social givens. It is partly this new situation that forces us to rethink how and what churches can and should be. Although in this chapter we are looking at a theological definition of churches, it is clear that it is churches, both denominations and congregations, that need to respond to this changed situation by deciding how to be. Churches need to decide how to be churches.

NOTES

1. This usage of agape owes much to the influence of Anders Nygren, *Agape and Eros: A Study of the Christian Idea of Life* (New York: Macmillan, 1932).

2. See James Barr, "Words for Love in Biblical Greek," in L. D. Hurst and N. T. Wright, eds., *The Glory of Christ in the New*

Testament: Studies in Christology in Memory of George Bradford Caird (Oxford: Clarendon, 1987), 1–18.

3. Ethelbert Stauffer, "ἀγαπάω, ἀγάπη, ἀγαπητός," in Gerhard Kittel, ed., *Theological Dictionary of the New Testament*, trans. Geoffrey W. Bromiley (Grand Rapids: Eerdmans, 1964), Vol. I, 45.

4. In what follows I am indebted to the work of Paul Tillich as well as to feminist scholars such as Audre Lorde, Rita Nakashima Brock, Dorothee Sölle, Carter Heyward, Mary Hunt, L. J. Tessier, and Judith Plaskow. See also Alexander C. Irwin, *Eros Toward the World: Paul Tillich and the Theology of the Erotic* (Minneapolis: Fortress, 1991).

5. This view of God is usually called "panentheism" and is the view espoused by process theologians such as Charles Hartshorne, Schubert M. Ogden, and Marjorie Hewitt Suchocki.

6. L. J. Tessier, *Dancing After the Whirlwind: Feminist Reflections on Sex, Denial, and Spiritual Transformation* (Boston: Beacon, 1997), 29.

7. Ibid.

8. Valerie Saiving, "The Human Condition: A Feminine View," in Carol Christ and Judith Plaskow, eds., *Womanspirit Rising* (San Francisco: Harper & Row, 1979), 25–42.

9. Martin Buber, *I and Thou* (New York: Scribner, 1970).

3. The Shared Memory of Jesus Christ

In this chapter I will continue to explore the vision of church that I offered in the last chapter by looking at what it means to talk of the "shared memory . . . of Jesus Christ." In the next chapter I will look at what it means to talk of the "shared . . . presence of Jesus Christ." In the vision with which we are working, "communities of eros" is a way to talk about the type of assemblages churches are, whereas "finding their common identity in the shared memory and presence of Jesus Christ" is a way to talk about what constitutes churches as Christian churches.

Although I looked briefly at those who affiliate with churches for social or political reasons in the last chapter, churches are not constituted by or for those reasons. Churches exist because of Jesus, whom his followers have called the Christ. To say that churches exist because of Jesus is not to say that Jesus established the church as institution. As will become clear below, I do not think the founding of the church rests on Jesus. Rather, the church as institution is "founded" gradually as the group of followers of Jesus seek to find ways to organize its life and carry on its mission.

When I speak here of the shared memory of Jesus Christ, I am well aware that not everyone or every church, denomination or congregation, remembers Jesus in the same way. The memory and the interpretation of that memory admit of much variability, and I will present only one way to name that memory. Nonetheless, as I will make clearer in the chapters that follow, there are many levels on which Christians, who might interpret the memory of Jesus Christ differently, might still make common cause from a shared identity because of that memory.

Relational Christology

In this section, however, I want to concentrate on how to locate the
memory of Jesus Christ. In so doing, I begin with the Jesus who is
remembered in the New Testament texts and with trying to discern
what is central to that memory in such a way that it becomes
usable today.

Memory of Jesus Christ is not memory of an isolated historical
figure but of the relationships formed between Jesus and those who
encountered him. This is a relational Christology, one that remembers and portrays the importance of Jesus in and through the witness of those on whom he had an effect. It redefines the locus of
Christology so that it is not in Jesus in himself, but in the interstices
between Jesus and his earliest followers. This allows for a refocused
look at traditional christological questions and answers and attends
in a helpful way to some concerns about Christology.

In this relational Christology, the question, Which is the normative Jesus? is not answered by reference to some supposed "historical Jesus" who cannot, in my view, be recovered from behind the
texts, but by reference to the texts that recount the effect of Jesus on
those earliest followers who encountered him.[1] "Jesus" is always
"the Jesus to whom certain people responded in faith and then
remembered and communicated that faith to others"; or "the Jesus
who evoked a particular response from those earliest witnesses."
Thus, any claims we make about Jesus—for example, that Jesus is
the Christ or the Savior—are claims about this Jesus and no other.

To begin with this Jesus is to begin with the Synoptic texts. This
is not the same beginning point as that, for example, of Elisabeth
Schüssler Fiorenza, who begins with a different norm (the *ekklēsia*
of women) and a different assumption (that the christological
importance of Jesus is his leadership in one of many messianic
movements of his time, a movement for the *basilēa*, a movement
that included men and women). I begin with the assumption that,
because Christianity is a movement that grew up around Jesus, one
can understand what is truly and centrally Christian only by
recourse to Jesus, and thus, that at least one norm for Christian theology must be derived from him.[2] In the end, I hope it will be clear
that, although Elisabeth Schüssler Fiorenza and I have different
ways of coming at the question of norms for Christian theology, our

goals are the same—to create in the present an ecclesial reality that does not inscribe and perpetuate what she aptly calls "kyriarchy."[3]

Both Rita Nakashima Brock in *Journeys by Heart* and Mary Grey in *Feminism, Redemption and the Christian Tradition* propose relational Christologies. Brock thinks that we need to move beyond Jesus to see the "full incarnation of God/dess in life-giving relationships."[4] For her, a narrow focus on Jesus misses the importance of seeing/experiencing Christ in what she calls the Christa/community in relationships where erotic power, the power of our interrelatedness, heals brokenheartedness. Erotic power incarnates the divine Eros.

In the end, Brock does not see Jesus as central to Christianity; Jesus is only one actor in the possibility of healing brokenheartedness. Her focus is on the Christa/community alone as the locus of relational healing. And, although here I argue that the community is crucial to understanding Jesus' importance, Jesus is not, in my view, an incidental actor in this process but is, for Christians, its central focus. Additionally, Brock does not grapple with the problem of sin and evil as systemic and difficult to uproot.

For Grey, the importance of relation is the importance of Jesus' relation to God that we can emulate. Here she stresses the example of Jesus and, in particular, the example of Jesus' suffering, which we seem to be called to replicate. Grey sees "mutuality-in-relating" as "the key to Jesus' developing personality, self-awareness and relationships with the men, women and children of his life, as well as the drive to his understanding of his mission to save the world."[5] Grey thinks Jesus "grew into the fullness of redemption."[6] Grey focuses on Jesus more than does Brock, for she sees mutuality in relating as breaking through in the life of Jesus and setting redemption in motion for the Christian tradition. Grey also emphasizes voluntary suffering as a way to attain more just forms of relationship.

Although both Brock and Grey see relationship as central to understanding Christology, the locus of the relationship is, in my view, misplaced for both. The critical locus of relational Christology is neither the relation of Jesus to God nor the relation of believer to community, but, first and foremost, the relation of earliest believers to Jesus.

The relational Christology that I am proposing makes it clear that Christian interest in Jesus is not an interest in an isolated and de-contextualized Jesus whose words and acts may be discerned with historical certainty, but in a Jesus whose context is crucial to his significance. We can begin to see the intertwining of present and past understandings of Jesus. Present understanding of Jesus is important because those of the past reacted and responded to him in certain ways. Present understanding depends, for its existence, on the faith of early followers. Just as there would be no Christian movement without Jesus, neither would there be such a movement without the response of the earliest believers. However much our present contexts may push us to look at Jesus again and to reinterpret him for our time (and we will examine this further below), and however important present context is for understanding him, we have no access to him at all except through the earliest witnesses of faith that gave rise eventually both to the biblical texts and to the continuing community that came to be the Christian church.

To look to the earliest layers of witness to Jesus is not to look for a pseudo-scientific objectivity as Elisabeth Schüssler Fiorenza seems to believe.[7] One does not look to the earliest witness to provide "proofs" about Jesus that would somehow otherwise be lacking, but to look for continuities between the earliest believers and later believers that would give indication that what calls itself Christian in the present bears some meaningful relation to the movement that arose from responses to Jesus. The earliest witness is about particular experience evoked and the continuities of that experience into the present. It does not ground or guarantee the truth or superiority of the witness; it simply places the witness where and as it is. Yet it does not make sense to me to try to separate the present from the earliest witness because the Christian movement began historically with Jesus and needs to be connected to its historical beginnings.

As the Synoptic texts indicate, women were among those first followers who responded to Jesus. To place the locus of Christology in the relation between Jesus and the earliest believers is to recognize that Christology is not first concerned with making claims about a male savior, but is concerned with the responses of women and men to this Jesus. One still has to deal with the maleness of Jesus, but if the locus of Christology is not Jesus in himself, but Jesus in relation to others, this puts claims that are made based on Jesus' maleness into a different perspective. If Christology arises from responses to Jesus, then Jesus' maleness is in no way central to Christology nor essential to his work, and no claims based on that maleness can be sustained.

Christology arises not from a man who acted "objectively" and unilaterally to change the lives of others, including women, but from the *experience* of being changed that happened to both men and women, creating a total event that was in turn remembered and communicated to others. This experience was, admittedly, an experience of *Jesus*, but its meaning is only given as those earliest followers found in this experience something that changed their lives. When, in the Christian tradition, we speak of Jesus, we delude ourselves if we think we speak of an isolated individual whose words and actions could be known and have meaning apart from the changed lives of those who first responded to him.

We understand Jesus' importance because the effect he had on others led them to want to communicate this to those who came after them. Such an understanding helps us to see that there is a very real contingency in the beginnings of Christianity. That the rise of Christianity depends in part on human responses to Jesus is an impetus to rethink certain views of the centrality of Jesus to human history and the coercive action of God in the world. It recognizes that history is the result of human choices and human freedoms, not of some imposed coercive will of God. The Christian tradition is a movement with historical beginnings, a movement that has changed over time. History shows us that Christianity is neither final and unalterable nor absolutely free-floating above its historical beginnings.

Understanding Jesus through the witness of others to him illumines our understanding of claims about the humanity and divinity of Jesus. In the tradition, we have often interpreted the Jesus of Scripture through a particular understanding of traditional language about Jesus that wants to make a simple equation between Jesus and God. Jesus is God, many have wanted to say. To some, claims to be "fully divine" are seen to be literal statements about a "historical" Jesus who, simply, *was* God. I am convinced that this view is in part rooted in seeing in the New Testament texts an isolated and context-less Jesus who *was* God whether anyone actually noticed it or not. Such a reading is often supported by searches for a historical Jesus and contributes to the notion that somehow faith in Jesus can be scientifically grounded or justified. In this sense, Elisabeth Schüssler Fiorenza's criticisms of misplaced objectivity are well-founded. "Its emphasis on the '*realia*' of history serves to promote scientific fundamentalism since it generally does not acknowledge that historians must select, reject, and interpret archaeological artifacts and textual evidence and simultaneously incorporate them into a scientific model and narrative framework of meaning."[8]

When we notice that we can approach christological questions only through the experienced effect of Jesus on others, we see that the central questions that Christology answers are broader than the simple (and perhaps misleading) question, Who was Jesus? Questions about who the first followers thought they had experienced and about the novelty and effect of their experience of Jesus arise before questions about who this Jesus must be for such experiences to be possible. Alongside such questions arise questions of how such an experience could be possible for others who had not met Jesus directly.

In other words, as presented to us in the early witnesses to Jesus, those who followed Jesus had experiences of grace, of healing, of wholeness, of being called from some lack of integrity to the possibility of fullness of life, and they understood these experiences as having their source in God. This experience seems to fit well the idea of flourishing and to include an impetus toward right relationship as I described these in the first chapter as integral to the contemporary human search. As Willi Marxsen makes evident in his distinctions between Jesus tradition, Christ tradition, and Jesus Christ tradition, it took time for the experience of God that the first followers had in and through Jesus to be turned into particular titles for Jesus and speculations about Jesus' person.[9] Christology is not first and foremost about Jesus in himself, but it is first and foremost about the experience of God's grace that the first followers had in their relation to Jesus. Thus, Christology answers questions about what contributes to fullness of life or flourishing and about the God who offers that flourishing as well as questions about the identity of Jesus as the one through whom that flourishing is offered.

Although I name the primary locus of Christology more narrowly than does Brock, in the interactions between Jesus and the earliest followers rather than in the broader Christa/community, Brock's view of eros is important here.

> Erotic power integrates all aspects of the self, making us whole. Erotic power grounds the concreteness of our experiences of empathy, passion, creativity, sensuality, and beauty.

Erotic power resides in the matrices of our connectedness to self, to the body, to others, and to the world. Through it we experience in the richness of our lives—in our bodies, psyches, and spirits—the flowering of ourselves and our worlds. . . .

Unlike agape, which is often defined as a disinterested, or objective form of love, most exemplified in the dispassionate divine love, Eros connotes intimacy through the subjective engagement of the whole self in a relationship.[10]

The relationships between Jesus and his earliest followers could well be described as relationships of eros, where connection and integration are paramount and where passionate mutuality is a defining characteristic. This does not mean that Jesus becomes a solitary "heroic figure"[11] who accomplishes all salvation through himself, but it does mean that for Christians, connection with Jesus is the primary place where we learn about and experience divine eros.

If the relation between Jesus and his hearers, the experience of grace that they had in his presence, is what is important, this also influences the way in which we think about what it means to follow Jesus. Since the Enlightenment, and, particularly, since the various searches for the "historical Jesus," much emphasis has been laid on the example of Jesus as though the emulation of this example is that which produces or guarantees salvation. But because our only access to Jesus is through recounted experiences of grace, our central salvific focus is not on the example of Jesus but on the ways in which the lives of those who encountered Jesus were changed by grace. The salvation evoked through Jesus is an experience of God's grace empowering changed lives and drawing them beyond themselves. The texts are not meant to be a list of rules that, if we follow them well enough, will guarantee salvation, but a telling of the story of grace-full experience that can, in turn, be the agent of that experience in our lives.

Making Jesus' example or practice the central focus of Christology might lead to the same sort of objectification or pseudo-scientific claims for him that Elisabeth Schüssler Fiorenza sees arising in the search for the historical Jesus. If one depends solely on example, then what about situations that do not arise in the Gospels? There is no blueprint for a nonoppressive political system in the Gospels, although we can read hints from the changed relationships brought about through Jesus. Nor are there explicit answers to modern dilemmas such as the ecological crisis or the threat of nuclear holocaust.

The experience of those earliest followers leads us away from individualism. I am not nor can I be in relation directly to a Jesus who is unconnected to the community of faith. Only through the community of faith was and is the memory of Jesus kept alive. Even if I talk about a direct experience of the risen Jesus Christ, I know that this experience is an experience of Jesus only because of the witness of faith passed down in the community. This challenges an individualized religiosity, a notion that somehow I can be a follower of Jesus in my isolated individuality without any relationship to the broader world. If I want the experience to be one of just "me and Jesus," I have distorted its communal beginnings.

Much debate has focused on whether the earliest Jesus movement was a movement for political and social liberation. Before the Enlightenment we do not expect to see connections between the radical message of God's grace and the human actions that ought to follow so as not only to change one's individual life but also to change humanly created social and political systems that perpetrated systemic evils. Still, one can see that to posit the locus of Christology in the relationship between Jesus and the earliest hearers means a definition of salvation much broader than a concern only for my own individual salvation.

The relational Christology presented here does have an element of individualism. The grace made available is a grace to which individuals as individuals must respond. In this sense, salvation does have an individual focus. But this does not lead to an individualism where, in being concerned about my own salvation, I have no need to be concerned about others. Whether I recognize it explicitly or not, it is the faith of others, their response, that makes possible my experience of grace through Jesus.

Nor, at the turn of the millennium, should there be a narrow concern with the "salvation" of individuals as though that salvation had nothing to do with the conditions of everyday lives and with people as whole human beings. Those who responded to Jesus received fullness of life. Indeed, the texts indicate that fullness or flourishing took a variety of forms and was directed to the specific situations in which people found themselves. There was a vision of a kingdom, a commonwealth where grace, fullness of life in right relationship, abounded. Followers of Jesus sought to communicate that flourishing and its possibilities to others. Whether or not those earliest followers had a sense of the social and political implications of seeking flourishing for self and others in right relationhip, we, at this time in history, cannot pretend that we do not know that humanly created social and political orders systematically prevent flourishing and right relationship for many. This means challenging not only individuals who stand in its way, but social, political, and ecclesial orders that prevent it, challenging what Elisabeth Schüssler Fiorenza calls "kyriarchy." The political analysis needed is specifically contemporary and contextual, but some of the tools to mount that challenge come from the grace experienced as the source of flourishing and the impetus toward right relationship.

If the importance of Christology is in the human relation to Jesus, and if we can still be in relationship with Jesus in the present through the ecclesial community, why should the relationship of those earliest followers be any more normative than our relationship to Jesus in the present? Quite simply, because we would not know it to be a relation to Jesus *at all* if it were not a relation through those first witnesses. Our interest in Jesus arises only because of his effect on those who followed him and told others about their experience. Our relation to Jesus comes to us through their memory. Indeed, the community of faith throughout the centuries has sought to keep that relation alive by its emphasis on Scripture. As long as this religious movement called Christianity appeals to Jesus as its foundational moment and speaks of him as Savior or Christ, we need to appeal to our beginnings to see and understand if our experience of Jesus in the present is in any way connected with the foundational experience.

Such a focus on Jesus does not mean that one can or does encounter God *only* through a relationship to the Jesus portrayed in the scriptural witness. Some have shied away from claims about Jesus as Savior or Christ because of traditional exclusivist assertions that those who do not thus claim him will be excluded from salvation. The focus on relationship to Jesus as the locus of Christology is not meant to suggest that one can encounter God only in Jesus or that the flourishing offered in that encounter is not offered anywhere else. Rather, it is an attempt to understand the specificity of the beginnings and continuation of this particular religious tradition, recognizing that all religious traditions, whatever their appeal to more general aims, have specific historical and present loci. The call to flourishing in right relationship for self and the rest of creation that Christians have experienced in their encounters with Jesus through text, community, and spirit may very well be experienced by others as arising from specific situations and encounters in their own lives.

Thus, a focus on relationship with Jesus does not foster anti-Semitism. Christianity arose out of Judaism. Christians have often contributed to anti-Semitism in the name of Christianity. One does not have to seek to establish that Jesus was atypical to his time or his religious background in relation to women or to anything else to understand the possibility of a movement growing up around him where people commend their experience with and through him to others and where eventually explicit claims about him arise.[12] The fact that this figure gave rise to a particular historical movement that has sustained itself over time does not mean that one has to argue either for the superiority of this figure or for the superiority over Judaism of the religion to which he gave rise. Claims about Jesus as experienced by his earliest followers and about the salvation found through this experience do not need to rest on some notion of superiority or exclusivity.

Does a relational Christology have any political power? Does it challenge kyriarchy? Admittedly, such a christological locus does not see the challenge to kyriarchy arising from the direct political involvements of Jesus or his earliest followers. The connection is both more indirect and more contextualized. Whether or not the early Jesus movement was a movement for political emancipation is not as crucial for action in the present as is knowing that the fullness of life invoked and evoked by Jesus has inescapably political implications in the present that force the challenge of kyriarchy in the name of right relationship or fall short of their fullest ramifications.

The relationship evoked by Jesus is one that calls for fullness of life, not just for the few, but for all. In the late twentieth century we are aware of the ways in which humanly created social and political systems (including ecclesial systems) order the lives of those within them, often to the advantage of the few and the disadvantage of the many. The fullness of life that is central to the Christian witness of faith cannot be attained without, in the present, challenging political and social systems that make such fullness of life impossible or difficult. Such a challenge does not depend on knowing either what a "historical Jesus" did, or on knowing the political actions of an early Jesus movement, but on a message of fullness of existence for all and an analysis of the present situation that does not overlook any of the barriers, personal or political, to that fullness of existence, on flourishing and right relationship.

The early Jesus movement did include women and men and was addressed to all as interpreters and experiencers, not just to some. As the movement is recalled and passed on by early followers, its earliest manifestations show no signs of following an established order of domination and subordination. The message was one of grace and demand—the experience of the grace of God as the force empowering the possibility of fullness of life, the demand that one live out that fullness of life in relation to both God and others.

In the Synoptic Gospels, one does not find any sense of a clear-cut organizational structure for the *ecclesia* that grows up from Jesus' followers. One can find only the beginnings of ecclesiastical structuring in the latest New Testament writings, and even then these do not seem to be unambiguous. My view is that the apostolicity of the church is guaranteed by fidelity to the gospel message, not by an unbroken succession of the laying on of hands. No particular structure is, in my view, either divinely given or dominically instituted.

Many different church structures might be appropriate as long as they respect the egalitarian nature of the Christian call to response, as long as they embody the salvation extended to all by God's grace through Jesus Christ. Church structure, then, should depend first on embodying the gospel call and message, and second on the particular needs of a given ecclesiastical community. Because of the exigencies of historical existence, the church is not one church but many. Although this might be lamented from the point of view of the desire for unity, the different churches, separated through history, now often fulfill different functions and meet different human needs by their tone and character.

To look to the earliest witness of faith rather than to the whole of the New Testament, or even to the whole of the Gospels, may seem reductionistic to some. Seeing that earliest witness as normative does not mean ignoring later reflections on that witness that might well illuminate it in ways that give us depth and insight into what it means to be in relationship to Jesus. I look to the earliest witness because it allows us to get as close as possible to the experiences of those earliest followers, and I regard those experiences as that on which the rest of the tradition is based and which it interprets. Even reflections on the empty tomb or the appearances of the risen Jesus depend, in my view, on the prior recognition of the importance of others' experiences of Jesus during his lifetime. Not all that can or ought to be said of Jesus or of the relation of others to him is contained in the earliest witness. But unless what is said accords with the earliest witness, and by this I mean reflects the kind of experience and relationship evoked in that earliest witness, then we run the risk of being cut off from our historical and experiential roots, and our way of defining the tradition comes only from our present circumstances and questions, ignoring our past. This would mean, on the one hand, that one can fairly easily rid a tradition of its most oppressive elements, for none of its traditional elements is essential. On the other hand, however, this means that there is nothing central to the tradition itself that can be used to challenge more oppressive forms of that tradition.

To see the locus of Christology in the relationship between Jesus and his earliest witnesses forces us to look beyond an isolated male savior figure to the complexity and richness of our own relationships with God, with Jesus, and with others. Such a christological locus presents grace as relational, grace offered and accepted. Relational Christology does not rob Christology of its political implications; indeed, it recognizes the power of relationship to God through Jesus to evoke change. A Christology of relation challenges patriarchy and kyriarchy while still acknowledging the centrality of Jesus to ongoing Christian tradition.

Shared Memory

The community of Jesus Christ, become the church, maintains his memory. Some of the memories of Jesus' relationships with others are recorded and interpreted in the New Testament texts. This memory is further interpreted by centuries of Christian tradition and preaching. The memory *is in* the interpretation.

One of the reasons that I point to the relational nature of Christology is to remind us that we are not dealing with "facts" but with meaning. The effect of Jesus is what we remember and pass on to future generations. Thus, even though we cannot get back to

Jesus' exact words and deeds, we do have access to how those who responded experienced him.

Memory is not the same as empirical history. Often as we are growing up we hear family stories about the time when this or that happened. As children we begin to tell our own stories to others or pass the family stories along. The important stories, the ones that get remembered and passed on through generations, are usually important because they say something about who the family is and how it understands itself. But when they are told they are not always told in exactly the same way. Each teller adds something and tells it from a different point of view. Yet the story still illuminates the family, even if the teller is generations from the event.

Keeping the memory of Jesus alive is like telling the story over and over again while allowing that the telling takes on different forms and emphases over time and space. If the story is not kept alive in community, it ceases to be of current relevance and becomes an ossified story without a living purpose. The church is the guardian of the story. As to all guardians, there are different ways available to the church to watch over the story. The story can be preserved in a glass case, hermetically sealed off from the lives of those it is supposed to reach, or it can become part of the story of others as they integrate it into their lives.

Churches are extensions of the relationship to Jesus that was had by the earliest followers. They extend this relationship partly through memory. Through communally remembering Jesus, churches allow for the possibility of continued relationship with Jesus on the part of its members.

Although churches may be and do a wide variety of things, it is through their connection with Jesus whom Christians name "Christ" that they are distinguished from all other communities that may engage in some of the same tasks. Even though the memory of Jesus may be told and proclaimed differently in different church contexts, the memory itself is shared and central to the churches' existence. So, churches are those institutions whose reason for being is Jesus Christ.

Identity is a complex matter, however, and the shared memory of Jesus Christ is kept alive in many and varied ways. Varied interpretations of the memory and varying interactions of that memory with the contextual realities in which churches have found themselves have, over time, produced historical, denominational, geographical, cultural, congregational, and numerous other variants.

Churches keep the memory of Jesus Christ alive through proclamation of the Bible and through interpreting the biblical texts in preaching and teaching. We will explore these as means of memory in later chapters. In the next chapter, however, we will turn to the continued active presence of Jesus Christ within the churches.

NOTES

1. See my *Feminist Theology/Christian Theology: In Search of Method* (Minneapolis: Fortress, 1990), 83–84.

2. See ibid., 78–79.

3. Elisabeth Schüssler Fiorenza defines "kyriarchy" as "the rule of the emperor/master/lord/father/husband over his subordinates." See *Jesus, Miriam's Child, Sophia's Prophet: Critical Issues in Feminist Christology* (New York: Continuum, 1994), 14.

4. Rita Nakashima Brock, *Journeys by Heart: A Christology of Erotic Power* (New York: Crossroad, 1988), iii.

5. Mary Grey, *Feminism, Redemption and the Christian Tradition* (Mystic, Conn.: Twenty-Third Publications, 1990), 19.

6. Ibid., 120.

7. Fiorenza, *Jesus*, 75.

8. Ibid., 87.

9. Willi Marxsen, "Christology in the New Testament," *Interpreter's Dictionary of the Bible: Supplementary Volume* (Nashville: Abingdon, 1976), 146–56.

10. Brock, *Journeys by Heart*, 39–40.

11. Ibid., 67.

12. See Fiorenza's critique in *Jesus*, 82ff.

4. The Continuing Presence of Jesus Christ

Resurrection

Churches find their Christian identity not only in keeping the memory of Jesus alive, but also through sharing the continuing presence of Jesus Christ. To talk about memory by itself may lead to the notion that we are simply recalling a past occurrence. Yet Christians speak not only of Jesus Christ in the past. They also speak about the continued presence of Jesus Christ. One of the ways Christians talk about this presence is as the presence of the resurrected Christ.

Although the Gospel accounts of the resurrection differ in many ways in the details they present with the stories, there do seem to be three early traditions: the empty tomb; an angelophany proclaiming that Jesus has been raised and enjoining witness to that on the part of the hearers; appearances of Jesus to various persons and groups.[1] In this chapter, when I speak of "resurrection" I mean any or all of these three early traditions.

In the Christian tradition, when we deal with the resurrection of Jesus we need to learn to pose the right questions. Often, we have gotten ourselves into knots about the question, What really happened? without seeing clearly that this is the wrong question. What happened as a question about what, literally and physically, happened to Jesus' body is not a question that the Gospel writers can or do answer. The only detail of the stories that admits of historical verification is that the tomb was empty. As even the Gospel writers know, there are many ways in which the empty tomb could be interpreted or explained. Besides the empty tomb, the earliest traditions about the resurrection are affirmations of faith rather than detailed stories: "he has been raised"; "he appeared."

We can get no closer to the resurrection than to know that the way the earliest witnesses accounted for their experiences after Jesus' death was by speaking of the empty tomb, an angelophany, and appearances; what is important about all three traditions is the difference they made in the lives of the earliest followers of Jesus and those who would come after. To speak the word of resurrection is already to interpret, to speak through the lips of faith about what God has done. We cannot reach behind the experiences of the women at the tomb or any of those to whom the tradition speaks of Jesus' appearance. What we do know, however, is that, whatever the experiences, they had a profound effect on the fledgling community that had grown up around Jesus.

In the stories of the resurrection we can see very clearly that we are dealing not just with Jesus by himself but with the relationship between Jesus and others. There are no accounts of the resurrection possible without their witness to it. Resurrection is a continued part of the relational Christology presented in the preceding chapter.

We are not looking for facts, but for the import of the experiences of the earliest witnesses. In the resurrection themes of empty tomb, angelophany, and appearance, one central theme predominates: relationship with Jesus continues despite his death. What I mean by this is that those who followed Jesus during his lifetime, and soon others as well, continued in their following after his death, and they explained this continuance in terms of their experience that Jesus who was crucified was not dead but alive. As they had come to know God through their experience of the earthly Jesus, so they continued to know God through their experience of the risen Jesus. What resurrection means, therefore, is that relationship to Jesus is still a possibility for those earliest followers and for us. Whatever the first witnesses to resurrection experienced, which they told as witnesses of faith in terms of accounts of empty tomb, angelophany/commissioning, and appearances, they were telling us that their relationship to Jesus was not a thing of the past and that this continued relationship inspired them to particular ways of acting and being. We, through their faith, explicitly have access to the risen Jesus.

My position bears some resemblance to those of Bultmann and Marxsen, who speak, respectively, of Easter as the emergence of faith in a risen Jesus Christ, or of the cause of Jesus continuing.[2]

Insofar as none of us thinks one can get back beyond the witnesses to the resurrection, we are in complete agreement. To speak of resurrection is to make a statement of faith, and such statements cannot be independently verified. What we can see is the effect of resurrection, and that effect is that a community who had lost its leader continues to flourish and grow.

What I am trying to signal by my way of phrasing the meaning of resurrection, however, is that Jesus' cause continues precisely because those within the community, and those that came after, characterized their experience after Jesus' death as a relationship to Jesus continuous with their relationship to him when he was alive, by affirming that Jesus is alive and present among them. For those who accepted the testimony of the first witnesses to resurrection, relationship to God continued to be seen in terms of relationship to God experienced in and through Jesus the Christ.

Relationship with Jesus

I want to explore this central theme that relationship with Jesus continues despite his death by considering its theological importance under four subthemes that are connected to it. First is the subtheme of embodiment. The resurrection is a bodily resurrection, not a separation of spirit from body. Second, there is continuity with the past. The Jesus who is risen is the same Jesus who healed, taught, and was crucified. Third, in Jesus' death God is not defeated. Fourth, the community that grew up around Jesus continues and expands.

Embodiment

The resurrection of Jesus is in continuity with Jewish expectations of a bodily resurrection. The notion of bodily resurrection was part of the symbolic universe of the day. Here the empty tomb story is important, for it underlines that we are not dealing with a risen, disembodied spirit but with an embodied Jesus. Whatever has happened to Jesus, his body is vital to that. This view recognizes the importance of the body, the whole conglomerate of embodied identity that makes a person what he or she is. The stories of angelic admonition and witness also reinforce the bodily nature of the occurrence. "He" is not there but is risen.

There are many variations of the appearance stories and, thus, variations in exactly what sort of a body this risen Jesus is said to have. He is recognizable, but not always instantly. In some stories he eats and can be touched; in others he can walk through walls and cannot be embraced.

The theological importance of the Easter theme of embodiment is in underscoring the goodness of the body. In a religious tradition that has often lost sight of that goodness or feared the body and its appetites, it can be helpful to recall the embodied goodness of the risen Jesus, even to the point of noticing that he eats, not eschewing the needs or desires of fleshly existence. Affirming the goodness of bodily existence helps to counteract the dualisms that arise in Christian tradition where spirit is elevated over body and man as "more spiritual" is elevated above the "more bodily" woman.

Theologically, the ongoing relation of followers is not to some generic "spirit" but to Jesus. We know him in his bodily identity, and we know him particularly and specifically. It is his embodiment that assures us of his identity as the one who, during his lifetime, healed, taught, and ate with sinners. This is the same Jesus and not some other figure.

One downside of the theme of embodiment is the fact that some have seen the exalted body of Jesus in its maleness and taken it to indicate that male bodies are more spiritually perfect than female bodies. Such a move, however, belies the continuity of Jesus' resurrection with the general expectation in Jewish tradition of resurrection for everyone at the last day. Nor does the resurrection alone create this problematic, for anyone inclined to make much of the maleness of Jesus can appeal to the maleness of the historical Jesus before his embodiment in resurrection.

Continuity with the Past

In continuity with the past, the risen Jesus is the very Jesus who lived and was crucified; he is not some different figure. The empty tomb means that one does not have to contend with Jesus' body and, therefore, with the question of whether or how his body could be in one spot and yet his presence in another. In the angelophany/witness stories, the women are told that it is Jesus who has been raised. In the appearance stories, Jesus is recognized as Jesus. Even if some of the stories show a lack of recognition at first, all in the end turn on the recognition that it is Jesus who appears.

Resurrection, then, is a vindication of Jesus and of what he had stood for in his lifetime.

God's Vindication

Resurrection is about vindicating God's power and God's activity. The texts often use the phrase "has been raised" to point to the work of God in resurrection. Resurrection affirms that the death of Jesus neither defeats God's agency nor thwarts God's purposes.

The death of Jesus is catastrophic for his followers not just because they have lost a friend, but because it calls into question all that, in Jesus, they have come to understand and trust about God. The claims of resurrection are that God's love and God's power are stronger than death.

Part of the desire on the part of some Christians to affirm resurrection as an empirical-historical event—that is, as an event about verifiable fact rather than as an experience of meaning for one's existence—is the desire to affirm God's omnipotence over the forces of evil and death. The view of God's power that is operative in claiming access to what happened in the tomb and in the appearances is of God's power as total and coercive—that God can and does unilaterally accomplish whatever God wants whenever God wants to accomplish it. Therefore, to say that we have no access to what happened but only to its results is seen to put God's power and love into question.

If one's view of God's power is not as coercive, but rather as relational, the whole complex of events around crucifixion and resurrection takes on a different shape in relation to God. A God whose power is coercive could have prevented the crucifixion. Yet Jesus was killed, making both God's power and God's love questionable. Something like resurrection is needed to reassert God's power over the death God permitted but could have prevented. But if God's power is relational, a power that cannot coerce the freedoms of creatures into acting in particular ways but rather works with those freedoms and creates the conditions to maximize the possibilities of good, then the crucifixion is not something God caused or could have prevented. Crucifixion is the result of creaturely choices to act in ways that count against love. If power is relational, then God's power is not called into question by the crucifixion in such a way that this power needs vindicating.

The death of Jesus, however, whether or not it calls God's power into question for us, does create certain problems for Jesus' followers.

How would and could they continue to relate to the God they had come to know through Jesus? Even if understandings of God's power vary between the first century and the present, God's love is affirmed insofar as the earliest followers, and we through them, experienced the love of God that they had come to know through Jesus as continuing to empower them and to send them out into the world.

That the relationship to God in Jesus continues after Jesus' death shows that God's love is indeed stronger than death. In the ongoing experience of Jesus, the ongoing love of God is experienced and witnessed to. In resurrection, God is experienced as the God of life, the one who will be an abiding presence even after death. The continuity of Jesus' presence points to the continuity of God's presence among us and with us in life, in death, and beyond.

Community Growth
During his lifetime, a community of followers grew up around Jesus. After his death and resurrection, that community continues and begins to expand as it shares its message with those who did not meet Jesus during his lifetime. In the biblical witness, resurrection is seen as the catalyst for the community to go on. In the stories of angelic encounter in Matthew and Mark, the women are told to go and tell others that Jesus has been raised and will go ahead of them to Galilee, signaling that the community should reassemble there. In Luke, although the women are not explicitly commanded to spread the message, they do so. In the stories of Jesus' appearances, there are a variety of commissionings to tell the story of Jesus to others (e.g., Matt. 28:10, 16–20; Mark 16:15–18; Luke 24:45–49; John 20:23; 21:15–19).

Jesus' followers can go on because Jesus' presence continues with them and continues to be constitutive of the disciple community. The community that felt abandoned by Jesus' death is now rejuvenated in renewed relationship to Jesus. In that fledgling community, the experience of God that they had in and through Jesus is still available to them.

In addition, the presence of Jesus sends the community beyond itself to tell others their good news, the news of his life as well as of his resurrection. The continuity of relationship with Jesus beyond his death becomes explicitly available to others through the preaching of the community. Not all had or have an experience of the risen Jesus. That the experience continues possible beyond the ascension is part of the testimony of Paul. But through the community and its testimony to the experience that some had of the resurrected Jesus we come to know that experience for what it is, and we come into one possibility of relationship with Jesus for ourselves. One can continue to have a direct and immediate experience of the risen Jesus, which, as experience, does not need to be mediated through a Christian community. However, we know it as experience of the risen Jesus and not some other spiritual experience only through the witness of the community to Jesus' resurrection.

The Community Continues

The community constituted after the resurrection is not a new community, but one that is very much in continuity with the old insofar as that continuity is provided by the presence of Jesus. The communities clustered around Jesus are still constituted by Jesus, and, furthermore, have a job to do in telling the stories about Jesus and in witnessing to his effect on them.

Resurrection does not establish Jesus as central to the Christian tradition, and, thus, deserving of such titles as "Christ." The telling of many of the earliest stories about Jesus must have dated before his death because, as his crucifixion makes clear, his reputation seems to have spread beyond his immediate circle. Moreover, the Q source has no tradition of resurrection attached to it. Yet many scholars agree that even in the earliest witnesses to Jesus we have an implicit Christology that, as time goes on, develops into an explicit Christology complete with titles.[3] Resurrection is one more part of the christological puzzle, one more way to talk about the importance of Jesus for his followers. It re-confirms rather than establishes why such titles as "Christ" or "Savior" were appropriately ascribed to Jesus. I do not think Jesus' immediate followers believed in him *because* of the resurrection. Rather, resurrection allows them to continue believing through the continuation of their experience with Jesus. They were brought to faith through their relationship with Jesus. This faith is still possible for others through their witness.

It is important to note that what subsequent followers are called to through the witness of others is the same faith to which Jesus' first followers were called. Faith in a God of love who summons God's people to responses of love for God and neighbor is the faith to which followers are called both before and after resurrection. In the resurrection God's love is not experienced for the first time, but once again.

The main feminist work that has been done on the resurrection concerns the role of the women as witnesses to the empty tomb, the angelophany, and the appearances of Jesus.[4] Yet their role as witnesses is ambiguous.[5] In Mark (16:11) and Luke (24:11) the women are not believed. Pheme Perkins notes that without women witnesses there would be no tradition of angelophany announcing that God has raised Jesus, for there are no stories about male witnesses to the angel's message. She also argues that Mary Magdalene ought to be included in the lists of those to whom appearance of the risen Jesus is ascribed.[6] So, although the role of the women is somewhat ambiguous, their stories sometimes thought by the Gospel writers to need confirmation by men, their presence at all indicates the importance of the earliest traditions attached to them and gives women a central role at this important juncture in the Christian story.

If, as I have been arguing, the resurrection is about continuation of relationship with Jesus, then recognizing women as primary agents of that continuation is pivotal to understanding the tradition as equally open and accessible to women as to men. Instead of placing the male Jesus at the center, we have, as the focal point, men and women together in response to Jesus. Ongoing relationship to Jesus is ongoing relationship on the part of the community of women and men.

Through their witness and their actions, women are crucial to the re-creation and continuance of the fledgling Christian community. They hear the message to go tell others and they do that: first, explicitly the message of Jesus' resurrection and, further, other stories about Jesus that they know. Women are among the disciple community that had gathered around Jesus and continued to gather after the resurrection (e.g., Acts 1:14).

Although there is a risk of exalting the risen *male* body, on the whole the bodily resurrection, as opposed to the immortality of the soul, is useful to feminists as one way to counter the dualisms that arise in the Christian tradition. If bodies are resurrected, then they are good, not evil or unclean or subordinate to souls. Thus, resurrection of the body takes on theological importance in rebutting the devaluation of women as more "bodily" than men.

One can no more prove the resurrection of the body more generally than one can prove the resurrection of Jesus; both are matters of faith. But faith in the general resurrection is a faith in continuity with Jesus' resurrection. The God whose presence comes to us in

Jesus is the God who is present with us in our own dying and beyond. The message of the resurrection, that our relationship with Jesus continues, is a message whose possibility extends beyond our present lives. Resurrection affirms that God is a God of life not of death. Although we do not know exactly what it means to talk of a resurrected body, we affirm that we will be known by God in all our individuality and specificity, including our embodied individuality and specificity. If we profess Christianity, we will also be known in terms of our relationship to Jesus and his message.

In terms of the community of faith, we will be remembered, again in all our particularity and specificity, as part of the communion of saints present to those who come after us.

Spirit

Christians have also spoken of the continued presence of Jesus Christ as presence in the Spirit. It is both essential and difficult to speak of the role of the Spirit in human life. The contemporary interest in "spirituality" points us to the fact that people are wanting to affirm the link beyond themselves to that which is greater than themselves. But talk of the Spirit is closely linked with experience, both individual and communal, and therefore makes the question of discernment crucial. In Christian parlance, not all spirits are the Holy Spirit, the Spirit of God.

In the Western Christian Church one usually speaks of the Holy Spirit as the Third Person of the Trinity, "proceeding from" both the other two persons of the Trinity. In the Eastern Christian Church, the Spirit proceeds from the First Person of the Trinity. Part of what has historically been at issue here is the question of God's work throughout the whole world, not just work linked specifically to the Second Person of the Trinity, incarnate in Jesus. Thus, God's Spirit is active well beyond those who encounter Jesus. Yet, if as Christians claim, when one encounters Jesus one encounters God, the work of the Spirit and the work of Jesus Christ are interconnected.

In the Christian instance, the Spirit is the Spirit of the God revealed to us in Jesus Christ. Thus, for Christians, although we want to affirm the universality of the Spirit's work in the world, in nature and in human history, we also link this Spirit specifically to the event of Jesus Christ in the sense that the work of the Spirit must be in continuity with this event and vice versa. The Spirit, if it is truly the Spirit of God and not some other spirit, is also for

Christians the Spirit that witnesses to and re-presents Jesus Christ. If one truly encounters God in the event of Jesus Christ, the Spirit of God is at work here.

I have found helpful Karl Rahner's understanding of the Trinity as God's threefold self-communication to us wherein the First Person of the Trinity can be identified with "the self-communication in which that which is given remains sovereign"; the Second Person of the Trinity is the self-communication of God concretized for us in history in which God "'is there' as self-uttered truth and as freely, historically disposing sovereignty"; and the Third Person of the Trinity is identified with "a self-communication in which the God who communicates [Godself] causes in the one who receives . . . the act of loving welcome."[7] There is a "double mediation" to the triune God's self-communication.[8] God in God's sovereign self is God for us; we meet God in history in the one whom we can concretely love; we experience God as the one who surrounds us with love and enables our loving. Thus we come to know God as Spirit through the experience of being loved, being accepted, being welcomed into relationship and responding in love in return.

The Spirit is the Spirit of God, of the same God whom we have also met in Jesus Christ. When Rahner talks of the self-communication of the Second Person of the Trinity in history, he means specifically the incarnation in Jesus whom Christians know as the Christ. I have argued elsewhere that the concrete and embodied nature of God's revelation is not necessarily restricted to this one incarnation.[9] Here we are specifically interested in the relationship of Jesus Christ to the Spirit in the church; but Logos/Sophia, the Second Person of the Trinity as embodied in history, is broader and more far-reaching than the incarnation in Jesus Christ as was known even in the earliest years of the church's existence.[10] The Spirit is the renewing and enlivening presence of God in the world. To tie ourselves to a past event enshrined in a collection of texts might well have the impact of making religious life static and fixed, allowing nothing new into a tradition where everything had already been said and experienced. But texts need interpreting in new times and places. New questions arise. Life develops in unexpected ways. Experience of the Spirit, the continued presence of God in our lives, focuses attention on the present as well as on the past and guides in ways that help us to see both the continuity of any question or situation with what went before and the discontinuity that raises novelty. For Christians, to connect the Spirit with the life and impact of Jesus Christ means to recognize that the experience of the Spirit does not replace the experience of Jesus passed down through tradition, but complements it. The God revealed in Jesus Christ and the God revealed in the Spirit are one and the same God whose will is the flourishing and right relationship of all God's creation.

Through the Spirit we experience God's continued and continual presence with the whole of creation, not just with humanity. In the Christian churches we name and understand this Spirit as the Spirit of Jesus Christ. This naming is not meant to be exclusive; rather, it is meant in terms of self-identification. Churches who find identity in Jesus Christ as one who re-presents God and through whom we are called into relationship with God understand that identity to be continued in its experience of the power of God's continued presence in the Spirit.

Other Ways of Talking About Jesus' Presence

Many Christians have spoken of the presence of Jesus Christ in the sacraments. Throughout Christian history there have been varying interpretations of the sacraments, in particular, the sacrament of the Eucharist or Holy Communion, in terms of their relationship to the memory and presence of Jesus Christ. The sacraments have been seen as actions of remembrance; like reading or preaching the word, they call forth the memory of Jesus Christ. They have been seen to communicate the "real presence" of Jesus Christ to the faithful believer. They have been seen to embody the presence of Jesus Christ in, with, and under the elements without any change in the actual elements used. The Eucharist has been seen to be the actual body and blood of Jesus Christ, albeit through the transubstantiated "accidents" of bread and wine or through a change of the meaning of or purpose of the elements.[11] Whether interpreted as memory or as presence, the sacraments are a central way in which most Christian churches display and affirm identity and continuity with the message and mission of Jesus Christ. I will come back to the Eucharist in the chapter on ritual (chapter 7).

Some Christians have spoken of the church itself as the continuation of the presence of Jesus Christ. Here the image of the church as the "body of Christ" comes to the fore. The operative notion in the claim that the church continues the presence of Jesus in the world is that the revelation of God needs to be embodied and concretized as well as available in the Spirit. Although I would want to affirm the importance of embodiment and concretization, I am wary of claiming "the church" as somehow the proper heir of that embodiment. To me there is a vast difference between saying that churches witness to or take their identity from the continued presence of Jesus Christ, and saying that the singular "church" somehow *is* that continued presence.

As a woman, I have experienced at first hand churches as oppressive, as not enacting the gospel message. Both in history and in the present, I have seen atrocities and oppressions committed in the name of the church. Many churches continue to treat all women, straight and lesbian, and gay men as less than fully human. Even if we point to a distinction between the visible (institutional and institutionalized) church and the invisible (true) church, I think that the notion of the church itself as the continuing presence of Jesus Christ, rather than through specific actions and practices, raises more problems that it solves, especially in light of our task here, which is to talk about those who would explicitly ally themselves with Christian churches. My view of the church is clearly influenced by my Protestant background here, for, although I think communal connection and identity crucial to preserving and living the gospel, I also think that churches find identity in the gospel and not vice versa. As a Protestant, I do not believe that the church per se in any particular form or authority structure is divinely willed, and I find myself less and less able to refer to "church" in the singular, given that so many churches do not seem to me to be fulfilling the gospel message. Churches are the explicit communities of those who would ally themselves with the gospel. They self-consciously preserve and transmit the message and presence of Jesus Christ, but historically, "church" has been far too problematic to think of it *as* the continuing presence of Jesus Christ.

Protestantism was founded on the awareness that the church is at least as human and fallible as it is divine. Even though Protestants have done their share of claiming divine authority for fallible institutions, they have always returned to the recognition that churches themselves, although they may (and should) witness to God's revelation in the world, are not themselves that revelation, except and insofar as they share revelatory possibilities with the rest of creation. Indeed, for Calvin the church ought not to claim the authority that is God's alone. "Thus these sacrilegious men, wishing to impose an unbridled tyranny under the cover of the church, do not care with what absurdities they ensnare themselves and others, provided they can force this one idea upon the simple-minded: that the church has authority in all things."[12] It is through the Spirit, not through the church, that we learn properly to interpret the Scriptures. "The same Spirit, therefore, who has spoken through the mouths of the prophets must penetrate into our hearts to persuade us that they faithfully proclaimed what had been divinely commanded."[13]

Although Christians have had to grapple all through the ages with the relationship between those who are explicitly part of the church and those who are not, in order to deal with issues of revelation and salvation, these questions have become particularly pressing in the last century as we have had to consider the values and truth claims of other ways of being religious. In what has been called the "inclusivist" view of other religious traditions, the notion of "invisible church" has been important as a way to understand and include those who have not heard the gospel and yet are people of upright character and good will. Such people are said to be part of the invisible church, whether they know it or not, and therefore are encompassed by God's saving will.[14]

But if one's view of salvation is broader than restricting that possibility to connection to the Christian church, or even to the revelation of God in Jesus Christ, the need to somehow place all the saved within the church diminishes. If one affirms the possibility that God is at work in a vast variety of ways for the salvation of all humanity, then there is no need to convert all humanity to the gospel message. The communication of the gospel and the life of the church become, for Christians, not a matter of saving the world, but a matter of telling others the particular version of the good news about God's relationship with the world that is theirs to tell.

When I speak of the "shared memory and presence of Jesus Christ," this bears considerable kinship to the traditional Protestant marks of the church—the word purely preached and heard and the sacraments rightly administered.[15] The Reformers were concerned with how to discern true church in a time when they saw the church as corrupted. What ensured that the church was church was not a structure or a particular person or persons in authority; it was the gospel of Jesus Christ in its twofold form in word and sacrament. Here I am in line with the Reformation traditions where the gospel is what gives churches their identity and guarantees their continuation. Later in this book we will look specifically at preaching and sacrament as resources for the enacting of the gospel. Both word and sacrament recall Christian beginnings and bring them to life for those present. In word and sacrament, memory and presence come together. Past and present point to present and future.

NOTES

1. Pheme Perkins, "'I Have Seen the Lord' (John 20:18): Women Witnesses to the Resurrection," *Interpretation* 46 (1992): 31–41, sees angelophany as an early part of the resurrection tradition.

2. Rudolf Bultmann, "New Testament and Mythology," in Rudolf Bultmann, *New Testament & Mythology and Other Basic Writings*, selected, edited, and translated by Schubert M. Ogden (Philadephia: Fortress, 1984), 39; Willi Marxsen, *The Resurrection of Jesus of Nazareth*, translated by Margaret Kohl (Philadelphia: Fortress, 1970), 141.

3. See, for example, John Dominic Crossan, *The Historical Jesus: The Life of a Mediterranean Jewish Peasant* (San Francisco: HarperSanFrancisco, 1991), 422–26.

4. Perkins, "'I Have Seen the Lord,'" 34.

5. Ibid., 32–33.

6. Ibid., 40.

7. Karl Rahner, *The Trinity*, translated by Joseph Donceel (New York: Crossroad, 1974), 37–38.

8. Ibid., 38.

9. See my *Christ in a Post-Christian World: How Can We Believe in Jesus Christ When Those Around Us Believe Differently—or Not at All?* (Minneapolis: Fortress, 1995).

10. See John 1, for example.

11. A brief description of ways of understanding the Eucharist can be found in Daniel Migliore, *Faith Seeking Understanding: An*

Introduction to Christian Theology (Grand Rapids: Eerdmans, 1991), 220ff.

12. John Calvin, *Institutes of the Christian Religion*, edited by John T. McNeill, translated and indexed by Ford Lewis Battles (Philadelphia: Westminster, 1977), 1, 75.

13. Ibid., 79.

14. See, for example, *Lumen Gentium* (The Dogmatic Constitution on the Church) as found in Walter M. Abbott, ed., *The Documents of Vatican II* (London: Geoffrey Chapman, 1966), 34ff.

15. Calvin, *Institutes* 2, 1023.

5. Living and Acting Together

Embodying God's Transforming Grace

In this chapter we turn to the question of what churches, given their identity from the memory and presence of Jesus Christ, are supposed to do. The view here presented is that it is the churches' job to embody God's transforming grace. Then we will turn to the question of how churches are to do what they are supposed to do.

I speak of the grace of God, rather than the grace of Christ, to indicate a consciousness of the universality of God's grace and the scope of the churches' tasks. Christians understand the grace of God and the grace of Jesus Christ to be the same thing (though, of course, others speak in different ways). When they embody or seek to enact that grace for others, they understand it to be from their own identity as Christians. But, as will be seen below, that grace is not always named so explicitly, nor does it need to be so named, as churches act in the world.

God's grace is not a thing. Grace is God's offer of Godself to us and for us. In grace, God communicates Godself to the world in love, in eros. Although for Christians that self-communication has taken its primary form in Jesus Christ, Christians have also usually recognized that God's grace comes to God's creatures in other ways as well.

From the human side, the experience of God's grace has been described in many ways. Rahner talks about grace as the horizon of our very being.[1] The grace of God is part of our human experience of transcendence. God, the omnipresent, is part of all experiencing. For Rahner, we can and do experience what theists call "God" even when we do not thematize that experience into theistic words.

71

Some would argue that God cannot be experienced implicitly because there is no such thing as prelinguistic experience, experience without naming attached to it. Unless it is named experience of God (or, alternatively, named in some other way), it is no experience at all.

For me, Rahner's view makes sense because I understand God to exist in Godself beyond my linguisticality. That said, Rahner and I would not agree completely on how to characterize this God and God's relationship to the world. I view God as the matrix in which all experiencing takes place. God encompasses the universe while also being more than the sum total of it parts. This is a view of God that is called panentheism. God is not "out there" somewhere above and beyond the world, acting on it but not affected by it. God embraces all that is, and is directly and intimately related to all God's creation.

A panentheistic view of God accords more fully than any other with my understanding of who God is: from God's revelation in Jesus Christ, from recounted human experiences of the divine, and from philosophical reflection on the nature of a worshipful divinity. A relational Christology, such as that articulated earlier in this book, implies a relational divinity. If the experience of Jesus is one that evokes healing and integrity, then the God to whom Jesus calls us into relation must be a God of wholeness. The God of Jesus, as portrayed in the Gospels, is a God of overpowering love who never gives up on us. This is a God who continues searching as for a lost coin or a lost sheep—a God who keeps offering grace long after the world has given up. The God of Jesus loves tax collectors and sinners and welcomes all who would enter into relationship with God. This God cares about the sparrow and the lily as well as about the supposedly important person. This God relates to what is happening in the here and now and embraces all in tender love.

This is not a God who is indifferent, for as God rejoices in the good of one person changing her ways, God also is sorrowful and judges those who do not do what they could. Grace is not indifference. It is a summons to live our lives in intimate relation to God, in eros.

It is from philosophical reflection that I adopt the concept of panentheism to name the view of God that seems to me to accord best with the biblical tradition. Because the biblical tradition does not present a single view of God, there are times when the philosophical tradition helps illuminate views. For instance, panentheism helps us to rethink the relation of God to the world. God encompasses the world, but also transcends it. Thus, our relation to God is not one of an external agent acting on something quite separate from Godself, but rather is more like the relation of mind to body, or mother to fetus *in utero*.[2] The images of mind in relation to body or fetus *in utero* are metaphors, ways to help us think about how God and the world are related. The metaphor of mind and body helps us to see that bodies, although connected intimately with minds, also have freedoms of their own that are not fully coercible. Our bodies do not always do what our minds would prefer. Cells sometimes act quite on their own within the bounds of their bodies. A fetus *in utero*, although it needs the mother for sustenance, also has its own independence and timing. The mother has some control over the fetus, but she cannot coerce it fully to do her will.

Reflection on the activity of God and on recounted human experiences of God can point us toward working differently with the concept of power. We have traditionally thought of the power of God as coercive power, the power to bring about a state of affairs unilaterally. But that is only one of the models available, for our human experience is one where, finally, we are free to make certain choices. We do not experience ourselves as totally coerced, forced into only one course of action. Of course, a number of factors can limit our choices, such as our history, the social and political constraints that surround us, and so on. But we do not experience ourselves to be puppets in God's hands.

Panentheistic views of God see God as interacting with creation in response, but not in coercion. If we see God's relation to the world in line with the mind-body metaphor, we can see God as one who influences the world-body but who cannot coerce it into health, given the freedoms of the body's individual parts, which freedoms cannot be totally coerced into compliance. If we use this metaphor, we can think of God as responsive to the world-body's needs, acting in such a way that the body is as healthy as possible. Or if we see God as the mother with fetus *in utero*, we can see that the created world has freedoms that are considerable and exercised somewhat independently of the mother, even if they cannot be exercised totally without her. The mother in her turn acts in such a way as to maximize the fetus's chances for growth and well-being. Of course, the metaphor breaks down at the point of birth. Another

possible metaphor for such activity is to see God as a good friend
who has our best interests at heart, but who cannot force us to act
in those interests, while pointing toward what they might be. In
such models, the world and all that is in it already is the body of
God; thus it does embody God's grace.[3] Although indeed I do see
the whole world as the embodiment of God, this embodiment is not
necessarily focused and explicitly named as God. Here is where
naming experience of God as God is important, for experience of
the world is ambiguous. It needs to be interpreted. Experience of
God as mediated through experience of the world includes not only
God's freedom and activity, but also the freedoms and activities of
innumerable creatures.

When I talk of experiencing God's grace in a way that is not simply an undifferentiated element in all experience, however, I mean
by that the human experience of belonging, of meaningfulness, of
being loved, of being embraced, not just by certain other creatures,
but by what is ultimate in the whole universe. This experience can
come to us through the traditional symbols or rites of religious traditions, but it can also come to us in a variety of sometimes surpris-
ing ways.

> To begin to see, a little,
> what they taught me
> of themselves, their place
> among the living and the dead,
> thanksgiving and the practical
> particulars of grace, and to accept it,
> slowly, almost grudgingly,
> to come downstairs this morning
> as the paper slaps
> the front porch, look up, catch
> the paper girl with her walkman on
> dancing down the street, red tights,
> jean jacket, blonde hair, making me
> love her, perfectly, for ten seconds,
> long enough to call out
> all my other loves, locate each one
> precisely, as I could this house
> on a city map or the day I found
> my son, swimming within me.[4]

Grace is empowering. As we experience being loved "perfectly," we in turn, however fleetingly it sometimes seems, are empowered to love in that same way. Grace prompts response. Even if I do not necessarily explicitly articulate the experience as one of "grace," or "God's grace," we understand what Bronwen Wallace is getting at, for we too know the power of that perfect love in our own lives, whether evoked by the girl in the jean jacket or by staring at the starry sky, and we too want to name our loves in response.

I speak here of God's grace, God's eros, as transforming. Neither grace nor response to grace is static. God's grace is not a generalized caring about undifferentiated creation, but is God's active love toward not only the whole but all its individual parts in an intimacy that we as humans can rarely achieve. God's grace is God's active will for the well-being of all God's creatures, from the largest to the most minute. God's grace is directed toward the particular here-and-now and therefore takes account of the particular past of each creature and the particular possibilities for its future.

I have set forth here the task of churches as the embodying of God's grace. But churches have not always portrayed God as a God of grace.

> Morag loves Jesus. And how. He is friendly and not stuck-up, is why. She does not love God. God is the one who decides which people have got to die, and when. Mrs. McKee in Sunday school says God is LOVE, but this is baloney. He is mean and gets mad at people for no reason at all, and Morag wouldn't trust him as far as she can spit. Also, at the same time, she is scared of God. You pray at nights, and say "Dear God—," like a letter but slipping in the Dear bit for other reasons as well. Does He really know what everybody is thinking? If so, it sure isn't fair and is also very spooky.
>
> Jesus is another matter. Whatever anybody says of it, it was really God who decided Jesus had to die like that. Who put it into the head of the soldier, then, to pierce His side? (*Pierce?* The blood all over the place, like shot gophers and) Who indeed? Three guesses. Jesus had a rough time. But when alive, He was okay to everybody, even sinners and hardup people and like that.[5]

For Morag there is a disjunction between Jesus and God. She experiences grace in Jesus, but that does not somehow connect to the God she learns about in church, even when the overt message is that God is love. On the basis of some things she has been told about God (i.e., that God has the power to decide and enact who lives and who dies), Morag concludes that other things she has been told (i.e., that God is love) cannot be true. Her experience in the church contradicts the message of God's grace.

Of course, God has been experienced, named, and described in a variety of ways in Christian Scripture and tradition. God has been seen, for example, as wrathful and avenging. This is the God Morag experiences in church. How can you say God is love if "He" kills his own son and makes people die? Morag decides that such a God is not worthy of worship.

Churches need to be both self-conscious and self-critical of the God they name and claim. Here I am naming grace or eros as God's central characteristic. But as we can see from the example of Morag, that means little unless we portray God consistently in that light. How can God be all-loving when God, as all-powerful, could have saved "his" son and did not? In the church we have often pro-tected God's power and excused God's seeming arbitrariness of action by claiming that God knows more than we do, so who are we to judge God's actions? But Morag, and I with her, wonder why we should worship this seemingly arbitrary despot.

In my view, God's grace, not God's power to coerce, is central to our experience of Jesus' message. In addition, I cannot conceive of worshiping a God who lets creatures suffer for some greater pur-poses of God's own, even though God could have prevented that suffering. A God who cannot coerce everything to do God's will but who interacts with everything in love is far more worthy of worship, to my mind, than a God who makes us all only pieces in some vast plan that we will never understand.

I understand the central task of churches as one of embodying God's grace rather than as might have traditionally been named as one of "saving the world." I do this for several reasons. First, I do it to emphasize that churches do not act on their own, but in response to God. If a church takes "salvation" as its central task, it runs the risk of forgetting that salvation is God's to bestow. Thus, instead of understanding itself as existing because of faithfulness to God, churches might begin (and, I think, have begun, in certain times and places) to see themselves as existing for their own sakes. When churches forget the source of their mission in God, they tend to make rules about who can be saved and how. They tend to place restrictions on who is worthy to belong or to hold office. They tend to narrow the scope of God's activities to the scope of their own activities.

Second, the notion of "saving" has sometimes been associated more with the "telling" than with action. Thus, instead of *acting* as one of God's agents by trying to embody the eros of God more fully in the world, churches have used a narrower model of communication and agreement. What I mean here is that churches have confused *faith*, both their own and that of others, with *belief*. Belief requires assent to certain propositions, as in the creeds (e.g., "I believe in . . ."). In belief, the content of the propositions is what matters. If you can't believe in a certain number of important propositions, you can't be part of the faithful. Faith, on the other hand, is trust, a trust in the goodness of the universe and an acting in response to that. Although faith is sometimes articulated explicitly as faith in God, one can trust in God without naming this trust. To put the emphasis on belief is to put emphasis on particular and often quite specific formulations of who God is or who Jesus is rather than on the experience of trust in God.

Third, saving has often been equated with missionizing, with converting others to explicit adherence to the Christian message. Sometimes saving has been interpreted anthropocentrically in such a way that the churches have seen their responsibilities only in relation to human beings. If salvation is all that matters and salvation is primarily for human beings, then the rest of creation can easily be dismissed as instrumental to humans.

Or sometimes saving has been interpreted anthropocentrically to mean that through the saving of humanity all creation will be saved. If creation is taken into account at all, it has often been under the notion that through human sin creation was tainted and itself "fell," and thus it needs the sort of redemption in Jesus Christ that humans need. The rest of creation needs to be protected from sinful human misuse, but I cannot believe that creation is "fallen" in view of human sin. Nonhuman creation is not sinful. It does not need to be saved from itself, but from us.

Here I want to make clear that the embodiment of God's grace that churches are called to is not quite the same as the traditional view of the church as sacrament of God's/Christ's presence in the world. The embodiment of grace to which churches are called is an embodiment of grace throughout the world, not just in the church. It seems to me that sacramentality is not a continuous thing. Nor is it something that can be coerced or controlled by human action. When churches succeed in embodying God's grace, whether in word and official sacrament (see chapters 6 and 7), or in feeding the hungry, or in any other way, the church is not itself the sacrament of God's grace. Rather, it fosters and witnesses to that sacrament. I have struggled with why I am so uncomfortable with the notion of church itself as sacrament. I see a danger that the church will confuse itself with the grace of God and will see itself as having the power to control that grace (this is a historically justified concern). In my view, the church has a rather poorer record than it ought of actually being a place where grace is experienced and communicated freely. Neither the church nor any other human institution can guarantee that it re-presents grace with continuity and integrity.

Churches learn to understand and present grace in explicit ways from their origins in the experience of God's grace in Jesus Christ and from Christian tradition. But Christian communities also learned from very early times that God's grace cannot be restricted to the church (e.g., Acts 19:23ff.). And at their best, churches remember that they do not have a monopoly on dispensing grace. Grace is God's alone to communicate in God's free love for the world. Churches are agents of that grace, but not the only agents. When churches seek to embody God's grace, then, they do not do so because grace would be unavailable otherwise. They do so because they have a symbol system and a variety of ways available to concretize human experience of God's grace and to present it to those both in and beyond the church—ways that might help them better understand God, themselves, and the world. God's relationship with the church is no more nor less special than God's relationship with the rest of the world and its institutions. It is only when churches succeed in re-presenting God's grace with integrity, only when they truly embody God's grace, that they become true agents of God in the world.

For churches, Jesus Christ is the central re-presentation of God's grace that they then seek to embody for others. But the grace is experienced more broadly than its re-presentation in Jesus Christ, and churches seek to embody this grace in a variety of ways so as to help others to understand the experience of being in intimate relationship with God. Thus, the job of churches, but not their job alone, is to seek ways to continue the incarnation, not just within the church, but in the world.

To speak of embodying God's grace is to point to what churches should be in the present and pointing toward the future. Churches are not museums to the past. They are made up of human beings who, at their best, are seeking to live toward the future, not just to preserve the past, unchanged and unchanging. Such a project of embodiment is complex and multifaceted and needs to be fleshed out.

Fostering Flourishing and Right Relationship for All Creation

What does it mean to seek to embody God's transforming grace? In broad terms, I would argue that churches are doing their tasks properly when, in seeking to embody grace, they do so by fostering flourishing and right relationship for all creation. Thus, here I will explore the final phrase in my vision of churches.

I use the term *foster* here to indicate that grace is neither a creation nor a possession of churches. Grace is God's, and the task of churches is to show forth that grace in whatever ways are open to them. This means that churches cannot hoard grace and mete it out in specified "doses" to whomever is deemed worthy to receive it. It also means that grace is not an exclusive possession of churches. God's grace, like God's Spirit, blows where it wills. Churches do not and cannot control grace, but they can be part of the way in which grace is experienced.

Embodying God's grace is not a matter of simply being, but of doing, of active praxis that seeks the best for itself and others. Grace is relational. From the human side, then, if grace is to be embodied as unambiguously as possible, it needs to be enacted. This enactment needs to be recognizable in terms that meet humanity's deepest needs, which are articulated in this book as flourishing and right relationship. What is required on the churches' part is an active nurturing of flourishing and right relationship. Grace needs to be celebrated and recognized for the gift that it is. We celebrate God's grace by celebrating flourishing and right relationship wherever they are found as those gifts of God that most clearly point to the graciousness of God's eros for the universe.

Sometimes the celebration and enacting of grace is explicit, sometimes implicit. When churches are being explicit about celebrating and enacting grace, they often do so in the words and deeds of the liturgy, where grace is explicitly named and invoked. But much activity that fosters flourishing and right relationship, although inspired by God's grace and seeking to embody it, does not explicitly name it directly in the context of enacting it.

In June 1998, there was a horrible explosion in the city of Montreal that leveled a shelter for the homeless and killed three church volunteers, one of them a Grey Nun, the order that had run the program. As a result of the explosion, three thousand people were left with no place to get a daily meal. I am struck by how I probably never would have known about this place directly and explicitly except for the tragedy. I am also struck by the fact that such a place where the homeless can eat with dignity provides a good example of one sort of activity that can foster flourishing and right relationship.

As the challenges to churches stated earlier in this book make clear, not everything churches do or have done fosters flourishing and right relationship. Indeed, even though in the last two paragraphs I invoke the liturgy and feeding the hungry, I am very aware that both sorts of activity could deny flourishing and right relationship as well as foster them. Both liturgy and feeding the hungry need to be done with flourishing and right relationship in mind in order to be embodiments of grace. Liturgy can, for example, turn into an ossification and glorification of power and privilege where the gospel message is not communicated or experienced. Likewise, feeding the hungry can be an act of drawing attention to those who provide food and of making the hungry feel less than human. No type of act is guaranteed to provide flourishing and right relationship. We have to be attentive to the *way* in which the act is done to know if such flourishing and right relationship are possibilities.

To foster flourishing and right relationship does not necessarily mean making others explicit members of churches. Although churches have often appealed to the biblical injunction at the end of Matthew's Gospel to make disciples of all and baptize all, there are other images available that better suit a time when we recognize the dangers of Christian imperialism and when we know our brothers and sisters who do not share the Christian faith to be good people, people of integrity with whom we can make common commitments to flourishing and right relationship even if the source of our inspiration is articulated differently. Images such as recognizing ourselves as one part of the body help us to focus on our own taking responsibility for responding to grace in diverse situations that call forth diverse responses rather than for wanting everyone to respond as we do in one single way of understanding the world. Seeking to convert the whole world has tended to lead to an emphasis on the institutional church and to ecclesiocentrism rather than to a focus on God's grace active in the world. Then the task becomes the self-perpetuation of the church rather than the presentation of grace. When self-perpetuation becomes dominant, we begin to worry so much about change that we take the church of a particular era and pretend that this is the church for all times. We ignore the fact that churches have changed over the centuries in relation to the times and cultures in which they have found themselves, and we try to make them static entities, preserved to keep them from corruption, but, alas, no longer living.

Others may be engaged in fostering flourishing and right relationship. Churches do not have to be the only groups of people engaged in such tasks. What is crucial is that churches, without giving up their inspiration and foundations in Jesus Christ or their understanding that what they are doing is embodying God's grace, can act in whatever ways are available to bring about flourishing and right relationship on a broad scale.

Fostering flourishing and right relationship has personal and political dimensions. What I mean by this is that one needs to attend to one's own individual and group flourishing as well as to that of others. On the one hand, churches have sometimes encouraged such an inward-looking stance that only the individual and those within the church are of concern, and then only at the level of a disembodied spirituality that separates the person or group from the world of which they are a part. On the other hand, some churches have encouraged activity that is constantly directed outward without grounding that activity in the personal or group relationship to the grace it seeks to embody. Those who seek to be the church need to cultivate an embodied mindfulness that itself takes its strength and direction from the grace it seeks to enact. (This idea will be further explored in chapter 8.)

In the first section of this book I articulated what people are seeking (at least in North America) at the turn of the millennium as flourishing and right relationship. I understand the relational Christology that I set out in chapter 3 also to be amenable to articulation in those same terms. Those who came in contact with Jesus experienced God's grace through him. They experienced their lives as changed, newly situated for the better. They experienced healing and empowerment to live their lives differently. They felt themselves called to communicate that experience to others.

The salvific gift of Jesus is the gift of God's grace accessible to people in a concrete and focused way. That gift was experienced as offering the possibility of fullness of life and of wholeness of existence. Admittedly, this is only one way to understand the meaning and the message of the Christian gospel. Perhaps readers will see it as circular, in light of the fact that the very needs I articulated in the first section of the book turn out to be met by the very gospel that I think is central to Christianity.

But the argument is more complex and interdependent than that. If the gospel is to have any bearing on Christian life in the present, it needs to speak to those who are seeking to see it as relevant. Interpreting religious traditions over time is a matter of looking not just at the past to find out what the tradition says, but to the present to find out the ways the tradition itself has changed over time. Tradition is not a static thing that is simply lifted, in this case from two thousand years ago, and dropped into each age unchanged. We know from Christian history that Christianity has always taken the concepts of the time in which it finds itself to make itself more intelligible to hearers. The first five hundred years of Christian interpretation, for example, made ample use of Greek concepts in building its doctrine of God and its Christology.

In my view, the question is not whether one comes to the tradition with current needs and conceptualities. One does. The question is whether the message of the tradition has anything to say to those needs in terms that can be understood in our particular time and in varying places. As I understand the Christian gospel, it has profound relevance to the questions people like my students are asking. I am not arguing here that the gospel changes totally according to the demands of the age, and thus has nothing constant. In my view, the constant is the eros of God that Jesus' first followers experienced through him and the demand for a response in kind that follows from acceptance of that grace.

But the gospel always comes in a context. Thus the question for churches is how to recognize and adapt to the contexts in which they find themselves rather than thinking their message is timeless and acontextual. Theologies have always been contextual, and in historical hindsight we can see that. But they have also always reflected the contexts of their writers, meaning mostly white, privileged males. Theologies today need to reflect and speak for a much wider range of humanity if they are to speak meaningfully to those who are engaging in religious searches at the turn of the millennium. In many ways, theology has been quite adaptive to this new situation, and diverse and multiple voices have arisen.

The challenge, however, is whether the churches want to recognize the contextuality of their historical theologies and whether they are willing to open themselves directly to owning contextuality. Churches lose the currency of possibility to comment on or make an impact on human life in the present if they do not recognize that the gospel has been presented in a wide variety of historical and cultural forms and that it is contextual insofar as it needs interpreting for present hearers.

Such a view does not mean ignoring topics such as sin and salvation or other topics considered central to the tradition, but it does mean asking how those might best be understood by hearers today. A good way to express the concept of sin, for instance, is to talk of experiencing ourselves and our world as lacking in flourishing and right relationship. We are out of right relationship with God and with one another. We tend to act in ways that make matters worse rather than heal the rifts. We cut off flourishing for ourselves and others. This lack of flourishing and right relationship takes many forms. Such lack is systemic as well as individual. We are born into a world where flourishing and right relationship already seem difficult to attain and live. For example, sociocultural and economic systems place some in poverty with virtually no way out. Women have traditionally and systemically been denied as many opportunities as men. Westerners have historically viewed nonhuman creation as an instrument to be used for human ends rather than as creatures with whom we must live in mutual flourishing.

The perpetuation of lack of flourishing and right relationship takes endless forms. We are not all equally affected by it. We are not all equally placed to make changes, both individual and systemic, that would foster flourishing and right relationship rather than destroy them.

What the Christian tradition has to add to this discussion is its view of and experience of the remedy for this situation. And, in

Christian understanding, the remedy for sin is grace. God's grace, for Christians primarily and centrally re-presented in Jesus Christ, is the key to overcoming sin. This experience of grace is vividly shown in the Gospels as those who met Jesus had experiences that changed their lives and called them to live differently in response.

In response to the human search for flourishing and right relationship, Christianity offers an understanding and experience of the world that gives a particular view of how things in the world are interrelated and how they are of infinite value. According to the Christian understanding of the universe, each thing in it, from the greatest to the least, is valued by God as its creator and sustainer. God desires the well-being of all God's creatures.

Human beings, who can predict some of the consequences of their actions on others and who have the freedom to choose or not to choose particular actions, persist in acting in ways that damage relationships between themselves and other human beings, between themselves and other creatures, between themselves and God. Moreover they create systems that reinforce these damaging relationships by consistently privileging some human beings over others, and human creatures over other creatures. I am thinking here both of institutions such as slavery, which virtually everyone in North America today would acknowledge as having been wrong, and of problems with which many of us have not yet seriously grappled, such as the inequitable distribution of wealth that is held in place by systems that make it difficult to challenge, or the inequitable distribution of power and influence along gender lines, or the way we tend to view the nonhuman parts of creation as instruments to be used for human advantage.

Both individually and systemically we cut off flourishing for others, often to amass more wealth or power or privilege for ourselves. And Christians do not seem less prone to such distortions of the world than do others.

Although churches have not always acted as if all creatures are of value, the tradition tells us that they are. It does this through its presentation of God's grace as encompassing all creation from its very beginning. It does this through the experience of grace through Jesus, who offered it to all he met, not picking and choosing the more valuable from the less valuable. It does this by its affirmation of embodiment in view of incarnation.

Not all ways of interpreting sin and salvation emphasize what I call flourishing and right relationship. Some ways of interpreting the tradition concentrate on the dualism of flesh and spirit, where embodiment is seen as suspect and as one of the main temptations to sin. Thus, in such a view, salvation is salvation from embodiment, from the temptations of the flesh. Some emphases on salvation see salvation as something accomplished for us in the life, death, and resurrection of Jesus, which will then be granted us as an otherworldly reward for what is believed and/or done in this life. Such interpretations of sin and salvation in my view see the tradition as primarily providing rules to live by. Grace is part of the mix insofar as it enables us to live rightly; but, according to such an interpretation, once one knows the rules one does not need the interactive relationship of grace that I have argued for here that enables discernment in each new moment.

Fostering flourishing and right relationship is the enactment of grace, of eros. It is highly context-dependent, which means it involves us in the constant task of analysis to discern what is required of us. It means we have to look at our interactions both from an individual and from a systemic point of view. The empowerment and the inspiration to do this task comes from the grace of God, available to the world always and everywhere, but also concretized and focused in Jesus Christ.

The scope within which flourishing and right relationship must be fostered is as universal as the scope of grace, which means it extends to all of humanity, both inside and outside the church, and to all of creation. Although at times churches have failed to take seriously that human beings are just one kind of creature among hundreds of millions valuable to God, recent Christian ecological theologies have begun to emphasize that it is a Christian responsibility to see all creatures, not just other humans, as the neighbors who should be loved.[6] Christians need to learn how to discern when anthropocentrism is appropriate and when it is not. For instance, as far as we can tell in terms of the creatures we know, humans are the only ones capable of the freedom and responsibility that would make the term *sin* appropriate. We have sometimes spoken of creation as "fallen" in view of human sin, and thus of needing the redemption that humans need. Thus, anthropocentrism in terms of sin seems to be appropriate. But in terms of salvation, what the rest of creation needs to be saved from is *our* sin, the sin of inappropriate anthropocentrism that sees all of creation merely as servant or instrument of human needs and desires and fails to take account of the value of each thing for God.

Although the task of churches, as I understand it, is to foster flourishing and right relationship, churches—universal, denominational, congregational—have not always done this. A lot of theology has changed in the last thirty years. More voices are being heard, symbols are being reinterpreted, possibilities for rethinking and for acting differently abound. Do churches want to change in response to the challenges both inside and outside their bounds? How would such change take place? What would such change mean?

In the final chapters of this book I will turn to some of the resources that churches have that would enable them, if the will were there, to take serious account of human searching at the turn of the millennium.

NOTES

1. For Rahner's view of grace, see Karl Rahner, *Foundations of Christian Faith: An Introduction to the Idea of Christianity*, translated by William Dych (New York: Crossroad, 1978), 117ff.

2. See Anna Case-Winters, *God's Power: Traditional Understandings and Contemporary Challenges* (Louisville: Westminster/John Knox, 1990), 220ff.

3. See, for example, Charles Hartshorne, *A Natural Theology for Our Time* (La Salle, Ill.: Open Court, 1967), 98ff.; Sallie McFague, *The Body of God: A Ecological Theology* (Minneapolis: Fortress, 1993).

4. Bronwen Wallace, "Particulars," in *The Stubborn Particulars of Grace* (Toronto: McClelland & Stewart, 1987), 110–111.

5. Margaret Laurence, *The Diviners* (Toronto: McClelland & Stewart, 1974), 77.

6. See, for example, Sallie McFague, *Super, Natural Christians: How We Should Love Nature* (Minneapolis: Fortress, 1997).

6. Ecclesial Teaching and Proclamation

We are living in a post-Christian world. We can no longer assume that Christianity will go unchallenged, either in its institutions or its theology. We cannot assume that religious searchers will see Christianity as the obvious choice. If the churches cannot provide what people are seeking, they are irrelevant. I think Christianity has the resources to provide people with the flourishing and right relation. It is precisely to the matter of the resources available to churches to meet the challenges I have outlined that the rest of this book will turn. What resources can churches draw on if they seek to speak to the human needs for right relation and flourishing? Unless churches can, in practice as well as in ideal, become places where grace precedes demand, the institutional church will fail to attract many in the contemporary world. I am not arguing here for a church where everything, every belief as well as every action, is equally acceptable and accepted. But I am arguing for churches and people in them that are continually struggling with what it means to be a Christian today.

Symbols can be rethought, and I have tried to do some of this rethinking in chapters 2–5 of this book. As have many other contemporary theologians, I have attempted to rethink our theologies about God and Jesus Christ in ways that are both faithful to the gospel message and more intelligible to people today than some of the traditional formulations of doctrine have been. My own brief summary of the central message of the gospel is that Jesus Christ is one who re-presents God's grace in such a way that those who encounter him encounter the pure boundless love that is God. The experience of God's grace or love in turn calls forth a response that we should love others as God loves us.

Not only does the church need to re-think its symbols, it also needs to re-present them and to embody their central message. My experience is that even though there has been a lot of symbolic rethinking done, my students don't get the message in their churches. It has not filtered down into popular culture that there are a variety of ways to think about theological topics. So, the availability of (dare I say?) good theology is not sufficient to guarantee that it will be heard by any but those who read theological books. Churches, then, have to decide how they will respond to these challenges by way of communicating, embodying, and acting the gospel so that the questioners can also somehow come into contact with some possible answers to their questing that might strike them as adequate. In terms of the challenges of today, churches must be truly inclusive of humanity; they must not privilege some over others because of race, ethnicity, gender, sexual orientation, geographic origin, and so on. Nor can they link themselves with societal forces that condone the oppression of whole groups of people. Churches must resist oppressive forces even when it seems beneficial for church survival as an institution to ally itself with Empire. Churches cannot any longer see themselves as the sole arbiters of truth and goodness by refusing to listen to other possible religious ways of dealing with human searching. Churches must grapple seriously with questions of sexuality and ethics in order to overcome dualisms that make us fear embodiment, run away from sexuality, or fence it round with rules so as to avoid talking about it. Churches must also continue to show themselves willing to think, rethink, and grapple with issues of belief and action. They must not try to pretend once-and-for-all solutions and must do so in ways that recognize that language is not timeless but context dependent. Thus we may need to abandon or to expand old ways of talking. Churches need to embody the human struggle as well as grace. They need to do this in ways that do not assume that God cares deeply only about human beings. Flourishing and right relationship extend far beyond the human community. As we well know, it is easier to say these things than to accomplish them.

In my view, in addition to developing interpretations of the Christian symbols that foster flourishing and right relationship, there are four main areas of life that churches have to examine so that they can meet the challenges posed by today's questers. Each of these areas of life offers much scope for meeting these challenges.

These are teaching and proclamation; ritual or worship; the formation of a Christian individual and a Christian community; and action in the world beyond the church.

Teaching

One of the tasks of the church is to express the gospel verbally. This is done primarily in teaching and in proclamation, or preaching. In the verbal expressions of the church, members learn how Scripture and tradition can be brought into our present time and place. Teaching and proclamation are hermeneutical exercises.

Teaching and proclamation, though both are primarily verbal in nature, are not the same thing. The teaching function of churches may be carried out in a variety of venues. It may take place in a church setting, such as adult education or Sunday School. It may take place in a classroom in a theological college. It may involve as learners both those who consider themselves within the church and those who do not. Here, we need to recognize that there is also teaching about Christianity that takes place that is not part of the teaching function of churches. This kind of teaching is also important for Christianity because it becomes part of ensuring an accurate picture of churches' teachings from a variety of points of view. Here, however, our major concern is teaching that is done, directly or indirectly, on the part of churches—teaching whose aim is, directly or indirectly, in the service of churches.

Good teaching is an interactive enterprise. It is not the imparting of knowledge from one who has it to one who does not, as though one were filling an empty vessel. Paulo Freire calls this the "banking" model of education, which he contrasts with "education as the practice of freedom"[1] that "enables teachers and students to become Subjects of the educational process" and enables people to begin transforming the world.[2] Peter Hodgson, in developing the idea of education as a practice of freedom, says:

> Such teaching requires an engaged pedagogy, that is, one that approaches students with the desire to respond to them as unique beings, that creates relationships based on mutual recognition, and that is also concerned to bring about fundamental changes in the way things are done in the traditional "banking system" of education.[3]

Good teaching is an exercise in eros. I would include here eros among members of the class, including the teacher, where profound connections are formed that allow, or better, encourage, the learning of all present. If the classroom is a place where flourishing and right relationship are encouraged, synergies take place that foster learning. Much attention these days in teaching circles is given to "deep learning," the learning that draws a student in and engages her or him in a quest for learning that extends well beyond the particular exercise or course.[4] Teachers seek to engage students with the problems that arise within the subject matter of the course in ways that require full participation and often group cooperation.

But I also think that eros is an appropriate way to think of the relation between learner and subject matter. Although the reasons for entering into the disciplined study of any area are complex, the sheer existential attraction of the area's questions and issues is part of why any student chooses to study. In the case of matters religious, or, in the specific case here, of Christianity, this makes immediate sense. Many of those who find themselves engaged in the study of theology, whether at the university level or at the level of interest, come to this study because they have religious questions with which they need to struggle, and because they have found, or think they might find, help in seeking some answers to these questions within a Christian setting, be it school or church.

If the love of God is, as I have described it throughout this book, an eros that meets and engages us rather than coerces and manipulates us, then the educational model I am presenting here is well suited to both seeking such a God and exploring the issues involved in a tradition that does such seeking. God is not static, but interactive. The world is ever-changing. Thus, no one set of questions and answers suffices to say all that can be said of God or of the world that seeks God. Knowing the truth that will set us free is far more than knowing a particular formula or the proper words to say; it is a lifelong process of engagement with God and the others with whom we share the universe. In my view, teaching in the context of a church or in the service of the church is an exercise in embodying God's transforming grace. As a teacher, I do not seek to embody this grace by providing the answers or by saying, "Look here, this is what I'm doing," but by modeling and encouraging forms of interaction that enable flourishing and right relationship.

One engages in the teaching exercise to help those present, whether insiders or not, see how, both historically and in the present, theological symbols have been set out and how theological questions have been framed and answered. Existential engagement also takes place, for students may well be struggling with their own religious questions, and theological teaching helps to clarify that struggle. One has a chance to engage others in the tasks of constructing contemporary theologies and wrestling with contemporary ethical questions from a Christian point of view. The goal of teaching is better understanding and engagement.

Theological teaching uses methods from a variety of disciplines, such as history, social sciences, literary studies, hermeneutics, as well as its own theological methods, to help people answer the theological questions that they are asking. The exercise of theological teaching, whether in Sunday School, in adult education, or in the theological college classroom, is an exercise in expansive exploration. All questions are permitted. All perplexities are entertained. Here the aim is not, in my view, to proselytize, but to explore. Although one may, indeed should, offer the tradition's history and answers as important parts of the data for thought, learning happens only when students and teachers together enter a process where neither the questions nor the answers are set in advance. Answers from the past are important, but they are not the only possible answers. Teachers at whatever level need, to the best of their abilities, to be able to provide the best possible scholarship available to them. That is, teachers must be constantly engaged in knowing where the growing edges of theology, history, and biblical scholarship are.

In theological education in any setting, the questions that arise from a particular context are crucial. What are the questions that people are most struggling with? What is the theological facet of these questions? Here also is the place where one explores the Christian symbol system, as I have sought to do in the second part of this book and elsewhere. What resources does the tradition offer in dealing with pressing questions?

Good theological education at any level is fully critical. By fully critical I mean to suggest that, in addition to all questions being permitted, one needs to explore criteria for what constitutes a good answer to any given theological question. Thus I do not mean to suggest that any answer is as good as any other. I think good theological education brings the Christian tradition of past and present into conversation with the present context and seeks to sort out answers that are in line both with the Christian tradition and with the present world.[5] Here, learners struggle with issues of truth and goodness, of what they can reasonably believe or expect others to believe, of what they should do or expect in terms of action from others. Here they struggle with whether or how the Christian tradition can provide a path that they or others could follow that would lead to their own flourishing and right relationship as well as to flourishing and right relationship for others.

In my view, dogmatism has no place in theological education at any level. Nor does the presentation of a single-answer-fits-all theology. If only answers are presented, or if people are not given the opportunity to pose their own questions rather than being told what the questions are, learning is seriously compromised, and learners often become convinced that their questions have no real place. Dogmatism has been one of the serious shortcomings in the church's traditional ways of viewing its teaching office. In the view of teaching presented here, the aim is to seek to articulate and to help others to seek to articulate for themselves the Christian witness of faith for one's own time and place, in terms of what one might believe and of what actions might follow, and of what implications this witness of faith might have for the daily lives of the various audiences who engage in teaching and learning.

In my theology classes in a university setting I often have students who are not Christians but who want to know something about what it is that Christians believe, think, and do. Such students pose excellent questions, both for themselves and for those who are Christian "insiders." In the process, all students learn something about themselves and about their relationship to the Christian tradition, whatever that relationship is.

I spent several years engaged in an exercise in constructive theology with a women's group in a local congregation in Dallas. Although the members of the group knew quite a bit about Christian history and the theologies that had preceded them, and although they were definitely willing to learn more, the aim was to help the women in the group put together and test out their own theological opinions and thoughts in a supportive and nurturing environment where there were no "wrong" questions or answers. In that group I learned a lot about asking and answering questions.

It is important, however, that churches begin to rethink who the audience in teaching is. For if the audience is considered to be only those who are already "insiders," then churches miss crucial chances to change popular (but perhaps outdated) views of what Christianity is. In its teaching role, churches have a chance to reach those who are interested in Christianity for a variety of reasons, but who would not usually be reached by preaching. Churches need to figure out how to reach those who might be interested in the questions or issues of Christianity, but who would not want to be indoctrinated into any one particular view.

Theological colleges are well placed to invite inquirers into courses, not with the purpose of conversion, but with the purpose of education. But churches also could advertise educational events for a broader community than just their members. They could hold open forums with a variety of viewpoints represented. They could facilitate discussions of timely theological topics in ways that the questions are opened up. A community near where I live has a Lay School of Theology that has operated every fall for decades. Each year they pick a topic and organize six weeks of study around that topic. The whole community is invited to take part. In fact, the theological college where I teach has often provided leadership for the school and benefited by having students come to us because their interests were first whetted there.

Proclamation

The exercise of proclamation has a different aim. In proclamation, which takes place primarily in preaching, the aim is to proclaim the truth of the gospel insofar as the preacher grasps it and seeks to transmit it to others. One does not avoid the difficult questions here either, but, whereas in teaching the questions are central, in proclamation the central aim is to re-present Jesus Christ to hearers in such a way that the hearers can enter into relationship with the Jesus presented.

Proclamation almost always takes place within the worship context of a particular church community. Proclamation is one of the main points of access to the Christian story. Although an individual can certainly come into contact with that story through the reading of Scripture, we always come to the reading of Scripture with particular interpretive apparatus, sometimes explicitly, mostly implicitly. We hear the biblical stories in our own context, and our interpretive context is partly given to us through the communities in which we hear the stories read and explained.

We learn the biblical stories in a context. Our understanding of what is central and what peripheral is directed by the context in which we learn the stories. I have argued that the stories about Jesus the Christ are the central stories for Christian theology and self-understanding, and that all other biblical material needs to be understood in relation to the Jesus story. I would also maintain that it is through the presentation of these stories that we today can come into explicit relationship with Jesus.

What gets proclaimed is a function of the ethos of the church (both denominational and congregational) and the choices of the preacher(s). The denomination forms preachers in its own image through teaching and through their own denominational formation. The congregation forms preachers by choosing those who fit their sense of themselves and by meting out praise and criticism to reinforce or to counter the topic, style, content, and so on, of preaching. But preachers are left, week after week, with the responsibility for proclamation.

The ecclesial situation of proclamation, because it is about expression of community understanding in words, depends on theological thinking. This is a situation in which it becomes quite clear that, despite claims that all Christian churches are proclaiming the same message, there are enormous variations in the gospel presented, from preacher to preacher, from congregation to congregation, from denomination to denomination.

What is the content of the gospel preached in this particular denomination? How does a denomination view the authority of Scripture? How is Scripture seen to interact with the contemporary world in formulating theological and ethical stances? Are there traditional theological emphases in the denomination? What has been the traditional pattern of preaching? How does a particular denomination view the authority and role of the church? Is preaching seen as proclamation, or is it seen as teaching the church's stance and rules?

In my own denomination, The United Church of Canada, there has been the historical Protestant emphasis on preaching from our Presbyterian, Congregationalist, and Methodist roots. Therefore, what is preached, officially speaking, is Jesus Christ. By requiring that all of its ordained ministers be educated, at least in part, in a denominational theological setting, that view is passed down to new preachers. But there is still enormous variance in preaching in the denomination. Many preach from the lectionary, but are not required to do so. There are many lay preachers who have had no formal training in preaching. If there are traditional preaching emphases in the denomination, they revolve around social justice concerns and the traditional concerns of the denomination for those whom today we would call "the oppressed." But such emphases may not be discernible in every context.

A few years ago the church prepared a study document entitled "The Authority and Interpretation of Scripture," which set a tone for congregational study and preaching.[6] This document did not lay down rules, but it did make clear that the denomination is not one that uses Scripture literally nor sanctions such a use in its churches. (This, of course, does not mean to say that there are no literalists among clergy or members.) The document is clear that contemporary questions play a large part in the interpretation of Scripture. The message of Scripture is not a singular and univocal message; it takes on different emphases as people read it in different contexts. The United Church of Canada does not exercise any direct discipline or control over the preaching life of the church, nor does it mandate that any particular stances be preached from its pulpits unless there is a particular reason to be involved in a particular situation.

The traditional pattern of preaching, the three points and a poem of my childhood, has given way to a variety of preaching styles as wide as the suggestions of recent books on preaching.[7]

The theology of the individual preacher and congregation comes to the fore in preaching. For, denominational stance and formation or not, it is the preacher herself or himself who consistently gets to interpret the gospel in a congregation. As a teacher in a theological college, I know that there is often a huge gap between what I hope my students will take away from their educational experience and what they actually do take away. For some, that gap is open and creative; they will move far beyond where I and my colleagues could ever take them. For others, that gap is one of retrenchment to the safety of a narrow and narrowly defined gospel.

In the congregation where I worship each Sunday, good preaching has been the historical priority. When they call ministers, they call preachers first and foremost. If I read the congregation and my part in it correctly, by good preaching they mean preaching that raises the deep and important questions and challenges them to think about possible answers to those questions. They also mean preaching that reads the "signs of the times" and addresses the scriptural texts contextually. Most of the congregation do not mind (at least occasionally) being discomfited, but they also want to hear the message of God's grace and love for them. Fortunately, they have at present a preacher who rises to the challenge the congregation puts before him.

I would argue that the content of the gospel preached must be consonant with the best theological work that is available in the time of the preacher. This means that preaching must grapple with presenting the gospel in light of the most difficult questions that are on the minds of people, both inside and outside the congregation. At the turn of the millennium, this means grappling, for instance, with how liberation theologies are challenging traditional points of view and what it means for Christian theology to recognize that Christianity is just one among many ways of being religious.

Earlier in this book I suggested some of the symbolic resources in the Christian tradition that would conduce to flourishing and right relation. Here I mean, for example: the priority and availability of God's grace and the challenges that it brings; or the importance of rethinking love in terms of eros; or the centrality of relationship to understanding the importance of Jesus. If the themes that dominate in preaching draw on resources such as these, preaching might foster flourishing and right relation.[8]

In North America, which has built many of its cultural symbols around biblical stories and which has been permeated with supposed "biblical" values, the culture provides the framework of interpretation. That culture has, in turn, been influenced by church proclamation. Here I am thinking of such ideas as the view of Eve as the temptress responsible for sin and the cultural impact that has had on women. Never mind that Eve is not portrayed this way today in all congregations. The proclamation that influences is often either from the past (one's "Sunday School days") or that which makes the most noise in the present via the media.

Proclamation can be abused. The abuses of proclamation have contributed to the challenges facing the church. Instead of standing in the service of the gospel, preachers (and churches) can distort it, seeking to present rules or dogmas rather than to re-present Jesus to the worshipers. Because of the form of proclamation wherein the preacher, basically without challenge at least at the time, gets to state what she or he understands to be the meaning and import of the gospel message, enormous responsibility rests on the one who seeks to interpret in order to proclaim. Enormous responsibility also rests on churches not to sanction the proclamation of a pseudo-gospel that fosters the aims of an institutional church rather than "seeking to embody God's transforming grace." Barbara Brown Taylor writes of three participants in a sermon: God, the preacher, and the congregation.

> What is called for . . . is a sermon that honors all of its partici-
> pants, in which preachers speak in their own voices out of
> their own experience, addressing God on this congregation's
> behalf and—with great care and humility—the congregation
> on God's behalf. When I preach sometimes I feel like Cyrano
> de Bergerac in the pulpit, passing messages between two
> would-be lovers who want to get together but do not know
> how. The words are my own, but I do not speak for myself. . . .
> As a preacher I am less a principal player than a go-between,
> a courier who serves both partners in this ancient courtship.[9]

Preaching, like teaching, can be a work of eros, of maintaining a vital intimacy and communication between self, others, and God.

In the context of proclamation, the gospel is open to serious dis-tortions. Thus the message itself, the content of the preaching, is a powerful tool in the fostering or prevention of flourishing and right relationship. Individuals have presented and churches have sanc-tioned imperialism, patriarchy, hatred of the body, anthropocen-trism, and any number of other possible themes that have been impediments to flourishing and right relationship. For example, churches have preached, sometimes explicitly, sometimes thinly veiled, contempt for Jews who did not and do not accept Jesus as Messiah. At its worst, such content has been used to sanction perse-cutions as horrific as the Holocaust. But even when such content is implicit, it is dangerous, as, for example, what might happen when one is preaching through John's Gospel and does not counter all the negative references to "the Jews" but simply assumes and preaches that one ought to "follow the gospel" in seeing "Jews" in general as people of lesser faith and morals because they did not accept Jesus.[10]

Not only is the content of preaching important to flourishing and right relation. The style of preaching is crucial, too. By style I mean how the preacher chooses to enact the proclamation. Having said above that preaching is different from teaching, I do not now mean to suggest that the preacher ought to be uncommitted to what she or he is preaching. If the job is to enact the presence of Jesus Christ in word, then one should not shy away from doing that. But that can be done in a variety of ways. To proclaim what one would defend as true and worthy of acceptance by others does not necessarily also have to be to proclaim in such a way as to convey that the preacher's stance is the only possible stance. Proclamation can invite hearers to explore their own thoughts and to enter into their own struggles. Although good preaching must have a point of view (as, I think, does good teaching), it can be open-ended and inviting exploration rather than closed and dogmatic. It can show how context might influence point of view. It can explore various interpretive modes. It can include listeners as participants in the verbal event of presenting Jesus Christ rather than exclude them by making them into a passive audience to be told what the gospel is. "The preacher who delivers airtight conclusions from the pulpit leaves the congregation with only two choices: they may agree with what they have heard or they may not, but they are prevented from drawing their own conclusions. The preacher has judged them incapable of that hard work and has done it for them."[11]

Preaching is one of the key places where people are brought into possible relationship with Jesus Christ. In preaching, the Jesus of the texts, the Jesus of past history, is present anew to the listeners, and they have to decide not only how to respond to the content of the sermon, but also how to respond to this offered relationship. To relate to Jesus in the present, one must decide how to take the stories further, how to enter into those stories oneself. Here, I mean that a listener must decide what to do in her or his own context in response to the message of Jesus. That means discerning how to act in love toward the neighbor in a specific context or how to help someone to be open to an experience of grace. It also means discerning when one is an impediment to the flourishing of others.

The question of who has the right to be proclaimer is also crucial in understanding the underlying messages being proclaimed alongside the actual content of the message. If only certain kinds of persons are authorized to proclaim the message and others are defined out of proclamation by belonging to a particular category of human beings (e.g., women, including lesbians, and gay men), the message is not an inclusive one, no matter what the words. A church where only men can re-present the gospel in word and deed presents a view of the gospel that does not allow for the full humanity of women. Proclamation cannot evoke right relationship if right relationship cannot be modeled in proclamation. Although one may carve out little oases of flourishing, women cannot truly be equals in a church that will not recognize their gifts of proclamation and interpretation of the gospel.

Likewise, a church where gay men and lesbians cannot be proclaimers by virtue of their sexual orientation is also a church where right relation and flourishing are presented as possibilities only for some, not for all human beings. Both in the case of excluding all women and in the case of excluding gay men and lesbians from preaching, the implicit message is not just one antithetical to equality; it is also an anti-body, antisexuality message. Because women are traditionally more closely associated with the body and sexuality than are men, women as proclaimers are experienced as more "sexual" than men are.[12] If one adds to that the possibility of a pregnant proclaimer, then one can hardly deny or sublimate sexuality, as has often been done with male clergy, celibate or not. Because of our cultural homophobia, gay and lesbian persons have often been "reduced" to their sexual identity by churches who focus on sexuality in general with fear and loathing. Therefore, excluding persons from proclamation on the basis of those to whom they are sexually attracted rather than on the basis of the complex of factors that make up any individual identity serves to reinforce fear of sexuality and of embodiment.

Churches can also exclude proclaimers de facto as well as de jure. For example, although class background or ethnic background might not disqualify one from proclamation by definition, churches often have class or ethnic identities that then serve to exclude those who are not in the dominant strand from full participation in such activities as proclamation. If all interpreters are basically alike in any given church—all or mostly male, all or mostly white, all or mostly middle class, to give three examples—then no matter how diverse the church, worshipers and outsiders may well be left with the impression of a monolithic entity rather than one that is diverse and varied.

Although proclamation rarely reaches those outside the bounds of the church, it is the event where those who are part of the church, on a regular basis, hear the church's gospel presented to them. If the content of the gospel is preached as an open invitation to right relationship, with God and others through Jesus, this challenges prevailing cultural views of the gospel as a book of rules. In good preaching, listeners are drawn into the struggle of discerning the gospel and taking it as their own, challenging prevailing cultural views that preaching is about communicating a church's stance so all within will measure up. If preaching becomes the kind of event where people are surrounded by grace and encouraged in their own struggles, they may, in turn, communicate the gospel differently to others with whom they have contact in their daily lives.

Learning communities and the worshiping communities are called to be communities of eros, communities where passionate love is exemplified. At their best, both sorts of communities ought to be communities of passionate struggle with the gospel and passionate commitment to discerning its truth. In addition, the worshiping community is also called to be a community of passionate commitment to the truth as discerned, to proclaiming that truth, and, as we will see below, to enacting it.

By way of exemplifying the sort of preaching that I am pointing toward here, I include a sermon entitled "No Quick Fix—Contextualizing Forgiveness," which I preached on March 26, 1995, at Chalmers United Church, Kingston, Ontario. The lectionary texts for the day included 2 Corinthians 5:16–21 and Luke 15:1–3, 11–32.

Sample Sermon

As a story about the unmerited and abounding grace of God, there are few stories as powerful as the gospel lesson read today. The story we call the parable of the prodigal son is one in which we can see graphically depicted the love of a God who, as our epistle passage for today puts it, "was reconciling the world to Godself, not counting their trespasses against them." I have often preached sermons on the pure unbounded love of God that never gives up on us even when we do not deserve it. Furthermore, I stake my life and my faith on just such a love.

But as I prepared for this sermon by reading over both the epistle and gospel texts, a number of times I began to ponder how this gospel text is often read not only to tell us of God's love but to enjoin us to follow suit. At all costs, do not be the angry older brother who has never been separated from the boundless love of the father and yet who begrudges this love to his brother who has once rejected it but who now seeks it again!

If the parent is God, the message rings true. The overflowing and overpowering love of God will meet our repentance again and again. If the repentance of the younger brother is genuine, the story also rings true. The broken relationship between older and younger siblings can be restored if the younger brother is sincere and if the older brother can bring himself to say of the pain from the past, "My relationship with you is more important than my anger; let's begin again."

But consider another story. There was a woman who had a son and a daughter. The son, the younger, said to his mother, "Mother, I am leaving home, and as the only male in this family, all the wealth is rightfully mine. You and my sister will have to fend for yourselves." A few days later the son gathered all he had and traveled to a distant country, and there he squandered his property in dissolute living.

His mother and sister at home were forced to eke out an existence by gleaning after others in the fields. The daughter turned to prostitution as a way to keep herself and her mother alive.

When the son had spent everything, a severe famine took place throughout that country, and he began to be in need. So he went and hired himself out to one of the citizens of that country, who sent him to his fields to feed the pigs. When he came to himself he said: "If I returned home to my mother I would at least have a roof over my head. The house is rightfully mine anyway. I know what I'll do. I will get up and go to my mother and will say to her, 'Mother, I have sinned against heaven and before you; I am no longer worthy to be called your son.'"

So he set off and went to his mother. But while he was still far off, she saw him and was filled with compassion; she ran and put her arms around him and kissed him. Then the son said: "Mother, I have sinned against heaven and before you; I am no longer worthy to be called your son." But the mother said: "Say no more. We welcome you back to share what we have, for you were dead and are alive again; you were lost and are found."

Now the elder sister was returning from a night of prostitution.
When she came to the house she found her mother and her brother
sharing the last of the food. She became angry and refused to go in.
Her mother came out and began to plead with her. But she
answered: "Listen, for all these years I have been working to support
the two of us. Yet when this son of yours came back, you immedi-
ately shared the last of what we had with him." Then the mother
said to her, "Daughter, you are always with me. I love you dearly
and all that is mine is yours. But this brother of yours was dead and
has come to life; he was lost and has been found."

When her brother heard that she had been earning her living by
prostitution, he demanded a share of the earnings and beat her when
she brought home less than he thought she could have earned.

I tell the story this way to illuminate the situation of the elder sister in this version, the elder brother in the biblical story. The biblical story does not tell us if the repentance of the younger brother
was sincere. Nor does it tell us how the older brother finally decides
to react. As I reread the biblical story recently, I was conscious of
identifying with the elder brother, partly, no doubt, because I like
to think of myself as the responsible one, not the one who would
squander my living and come crawling back home, but also
because I was struck by the profound ambiguity of many human
relationships where simply emulating the gracious love of God that
never gives up on us cannot only be difficult, but might well prevent integrity or wholeness for ourselves and others.

Two realizations impressed themselves upon me. The first is that
we are human and not God. The second is that the emulation of
God's love does not carry as high a price for some as it does for others.

Sometimes in the Christian tradition we have made a straight-
forward claim that because God's love never gives up on us, we, if
we are truly following God's way, should never give up on anyone
else, no matter what the personal cost. Self-sacrifice has often been
touted as the only Christian way to act. But human love is not
divine love, and sometimes, for humans, the cost may be simply too
high. Healing a broken relationship is always two-sided; the one
who has broken the relationship must be genuinely repentant, and
the one who has been wronged must be willing to forgive or overlook the wrongdoing because the healed relationship is more
important than the wrong done. Divine love keeps doing this

because divine love is boundless. But divine love does not, I would submit, always ask us to do the same in every situation in which we find ourselves. Divine love never gives up on us, but it also meets us where we find ourselves and responds to our need—in the case of these stories, not only the need of the younger siblings, but also of the older ones. Where my human offer of relationship is not met by true repentance on the part of the one who has wronged me, I have a hard time believing that God's love for me requires me to keep putting myself in the path of hurt. God's love, extended to the elder brother and to the younger, the elder sister and to the younger brother, seeks wholeness for both. If one spurns that wholeness, willfully and callously, I do not think that the other is enjoined by divine love to keep extending forgiveness at the expense of integrity.

In seeking to understand the love enjoined by the parable of the prodigal son, we should not lose sight of the fact that a different context might signal the need for a different vision of what is required. In the biblical story it does not seem that the elder brother would lose a lot by welcoming the younger one back. He does not lose his livelihood. By all appearances, things are going well. There is plenty of food, a fatted calf to kill, and servants to prepare the feast. Even if the younger son continues an irresponsible life, the elder will probably have to sacrifice little.

But the daughter in my story, or the battered woman, or the sexually abused child, has much more to lose if she hears only a message that says "forgive at all costs" than does the elder brother whose life and livelihood seem assured. In the Christian tradition, the preaching of self-sacrifice has rarely taken account of the fact that in the Gospels, the message of Jesus is profoundly contextual. There is no one rule for all. Instead, the good news seems to have taken many forms, yet always offers the promise of wholeness through the unbounded love of God. That love, responded to in faith, will give us the power, the strength, the determination, the love, to overcome what separates us from wholeness. We have taken stories about Jesus and his interactions with people in specific and particular situations and tried to turn them into rules for living applicable in all times and all places and to all people. In our preaching and teaching, we have often failed to see that relationship is a two-way street involving not only forgiveness, but a true repentance that can lead to integrity for both parties.

In Lent we focus our reflections on the many ways in which God's love for us is so powerful that it seeks reconciliation with us. We focus on the ways in which we thwart that love and on our part in reclaiming relationship with God and with one another. God's boundless grace and our desire for renewed relationship notwithstanding, there are times when renewed relationship is impossible because the other with whom we would be in relationship does not reciprocate.

Perhaps most of us here today need to hear the story of the elder brother told straightforwardly. It may be that most of us are not inclined to offer renewed relationship to those whom we think have been irresponsible, no matter how genuine their repentance, and that we need to be reminded that the grace of God desires us to meet repentance with forgiveness. But that is only part of the gospel story. For the gospel also desires wholeness not only for the younger brother, but for all the elder brothers and sisters of the world who have done what they could with what they had. When the younger brother comes home, self-examination on the part of the elder is definitely in order. But if the younger brother again and again betrays our trust and injures us in a host of ways, then the gospel message of integrity offered to both younger and elder may mean that some relationships cannot be healed. I worry that the Christian church has often passed over this side of the matter far too quickly and too simply. There are times when the integrity of the elder brother and sister may be more important than one particular restored relationship between two human beings. The gospel promises fullness of life. Discerning when we need to persevere in offering reconciliation and when the offer of reconciliation is so costly that we cannot be freed for life-giving relationship with God and others is the complex task of living the Christian life to its fullness.

The grace of God offers wholeness to both the elder brother and the younger. May it be so for us.

Now to the God who wills wholeness for all creation, who offers us that wholeness in Jesus Christ, and who, in the Spirit, empowers us to work toward wholeness and healing, be all honor and glory and praise.

NOTES

1. Paulo Freire, *Pedagogy of the Oppressed*, translated by Myra Bergman Ramos (New York: Seabury, 1970), 67–69.

2. Ibid., 74.

3. Peter C. Hodgson, "Liberal Theology and Transformative Pedagogy," *Teaching Religion and Theology* 2 (1999): 73.

4. See, for example, "Deep Learning, Surface Learning," *American Association of Higher Education Bulletin* (April 1993): 10–14; James Rhem, "Deep/SurfaceApproaches to Learning: An Introduction," *The National Teaching & Learning Forum* 5 (1995): 1–3; Christopher K. Knapper, "Understanding Student Learning: Implications for Instructional Practice," in W. A. Wright, ed., *Teaching Improvement Practices: Successful Strategies for Higher Education* (Boston: Maker, 1995), 58–75.

5. For a fuller explanation of how I myself would do this, see my *Feminist Theology/Christian Theology: In Search of Method* (Philadelphia: Fortress, 1990).

6. Theology and Faith Committee of The United Church of Canada, "The Authority and Interpretation of Scripture," 1989.

7. See, for example, Stephen Farris, *Preaching That Matters: The Bible and Our Lives* (Louisville: Westminster/John Knox, 1998); Charles L. Rice, *The Embodied Word: Preaching as Art and Liturgy* (Minneapolis: Fortress, 1991); Lucy Atkinson Rose, *Sharing the Word: Preaching in the Roundtable Church* (Louisville: Westminster/John Knox, 1997); Christine M. Smith, *Weaving the Sermon: Preaching in a Feminist Perspective* (Louisville: Westminster/John Knox, 1989); Paul Scott Wilson, *The Practice of Preaching* (Nashville: Abingdon, 1995).

8. For a discussion of theology in preaching, see Wilson, *The Practice of Preaching*, 82–97.

9. Barbara Brown Taylor, *The Preaching Life* (Boston: Cowley, 1993), 78.

10. As a counter to this, see Christine M. Smith, *Preaching as Weeping, Confession, and Resistance: Radical Responses to Radical Evil* (Louisville: Westminster/John Knox, 1992).

11. Taylor, *The Preaching Life*, 82.

12. See, for example, Rosemary Radford Ruether, *Sexism and God-Talk: Toward a Feminist Theology* (Boston: Beacon, 1983), 72–92, 193–213.

7. Ritual as a Resource for Flourishing and Right Relationship

When I talk to people who have opted out of mainstream religious traditions and are seeking alternate "spiritualities," one of the things that I have discovered is that virtually all of them speak of the "rituals" that are part of their new spirituality. Such people are apparently seeking a place where they can be active participants in individual or communal rituals, where they get to "do" something, to use their five senses in a variety of ways. In my experience they also articulate a desire to create places and actions that are aesthetically pleasing.

Christians have embodied their witness in ritualized actions of worship almost from the very beginnings of the Christian movement. If the main aim of Christian preaching is making Jesus (and thereby God) present to the people in word, the main aim of Christian rituals of a variety of sorts is to make Jesus (and thereby God) present in action as well as word. This is done through what James White helpfully distinguishes as "structures" (ways to organize time and space) and "services" (conjoined words and actions of particular liturgical types for particular occasions).[1]

Christian rituals vary among denominations and geographical settings and have historically been subject to vastly different interpretations (I think here of the various denominational views of the Eucharist, for example). In this chapter I am thinking primarily of those communal rituals that are common in mainstream Protestantism—in particular, patterns for weekly worship, celebration of baptism and communion, rites of confirmation. Funerals and weddings are also ritual opportunities. In thinking about ritual acts we will also look a bit at the spaces where ritual takes place and the symbols that adorn those spaces.

In Protestantism, especially those strains of Protestantism descended from Calvin, there has been enormous wariness of symbol and act without verbal interpretation. Calvin's aim was to avoid "superstition." He did not want the rituals to appear magically efficacious.[2] Thus, Protestant ritual has traditionally been word based with music as an important complement to the word. Since the ecumenical movement beginning in the 1960s, however, Protestants have begun to use more and more nonverbal symbols and actions to accompany the words of ritual as part of the general ambiance or specific liturgical season. Although it was very uncommon to do so in the church of my childhood, now in the celebration of communion the bread is actually broken and the cup elevated as the words of institution (that is, the story of the last supper) are said. Seasonal liturgical colors are common in many Protestant churches, and there is more use of the symbols of light and darkness for Advent/Christmas and Lent/Easter, including Advent wreaths and services of tenebrae. Other actions and symbols such as footwashing and the veiling of the cross are used in some churches. Some Protestants have encouraged oil for anointing the newly baptized or ordained. In many cases, individual congregations have developed ritual patterns and acts used over time in that particular congregation.

Within the ritual acts there are many symbolic conventions. The most common are the use of water in baptism and bread and wine/juice in the Eucharist. Rituals usually involve particular actors, set apart in some way to do the ritual tasks, and are often accompanied by special dress, music, words, hand and body motions, and other specific actions in a specific time and space.

What Does Christian Worship Do?

There are many theories about ritual in general and about Christian worship specifically.[3] Catherine Bell notes that there is "no clear and widely shared explanation of what constitutes ritual or how to understand it."[4] She offers the following general consensus.

> Today, we think of "ritual" as a complex sociocultural medium variously constructed of tradition, exigency, and self-expression; it is understood to play a wide variety of roles and

to communicate a rich density of overdetermined messages and attitudes. For the most part, ritual is the medium chosen to invoke those ordered relationships that are thought to obtain between human beings in the here-and-now and non-immediate sources of power, authority, and value. Definitions of these relationships in terms of ritual's vocabulary of gesture and word, in contrast to theological speculation or doctrinal formulation, suggest that the fundamental efficacy of ritual activity lies in its ability to have people embody assumptions about their place in a larger order of things.[5]

In Christianity, ritual (which is usually referred to as worship) has two major foci, God and the human community. Worship is for the purpose of and in the context of worshiping God. But it is also for the benefit of humanity, both those attending the service and those who are not. Thus, worship is said to glorify God and sanctify the human being.[6]

Worship is focused attention to God and to God's presence. God's presence is invoked often in worship, and God is addressed and spoken of in a variety of ways. In worship, God is expected, seen, and experienced as one of the actors. The worshipers' attention is directed toward God in a number of verbal and nonverbal ways. God is usually welcomed or invited to be present. God is addressed through confession of sin, through thanksgiving, through intercession. In sacramental acts such as baptism and the Eucharist, God's presence is symbolically embodied in water, bread, and wine. God is expected to be there and do something, and people are expected to be open to the experience of God and to respond to that experience. Worship glorifies God by noticing God, by being "set apart" moments in time and space where Christians concentrate on the God-human relationship.

In Christian worship, word and action have the potential to be not mere word and action, but enactment and embodiment charged with the presence of God. The story is told, but the story is also symbolized, for example, in the lighting of candles on an Advent wreath, thereby marking the passage of time through the season and highlighting various dimensions of Christian life such as peace, hope, love, or joy. In the Eucharist, for example, the story is reenacted so as to invite God and Jesus Christ to be present in the here and now. Worship is an experience in the present moment where, ideally, what happens between God and the worshipers is a moment of relationship, like a first kiss, where the telling is not the same as the experiencing. Thus eros is a good way to describe the relationships enacted in Christian ritual. The presence of God is invoked so that relationship can be forged and developed. Actions are often more powerful than words alone in Christian worship. Because actions allow us the possibility of entry into the experience at several points, the experience becomes textured and multilayered.

In ritual activity, often one act or one symbol can serve as a summary of the whole Christian story, a shorthand that brings the whole story to mind without necessarily having to repeat it word for word. The act of breaking bread and lifting the cup in the context of worship are self-interpreting to those who know the story and are familiar with the forms. If one had been to other Christian services, one could attend a Christian service of eucharist in any language and have the whole story evoked from those acts alone. Even without knowing the story, one might be drawn into the activity in such a way that one becomes aware that something important is happening.

One of the purposes served by religion is to help human beings struggle with ultimate questions, which questions are often the result of the finitude and fragility of human life. Beyond merely verbal answers to questions about the meaning and purpose of life and where one fits in the universe, religious traditions enact these answers, thereby keeping the threatening forces confined and manageable.[7] Christian worship is structured experience of God. There are usually leaders and expected patterns, which, although they might allow for much fluidity, are more than simply random acts. In the orderedness of worship, the forces of chaos are kept at bay and the order of the universe is shown. This is seen quite clearly in orders for the service of baptism, where water is noted not only as a source of life but as a potential destroyer. One baptismal hymn speaks of "Crashing waters at creation, ordered by the Spirit's breath."[8] Symbolically speaking, using one possible image, one dies with Christ in the waters of baptism and rises again. This is more or less graphically portrayed as varying forms of baptism, from sprinkling to immersion, are used.

Christian worship ideally involves the whole person. First, it involves an act of commitment just in terms of someone appearing in person, choosing to be present at a particular time and place. But it also involves an embodied response to a total experience. What I mean here is that Christian worship is more than just knowing or saying the right words. Even the words, when said, are not just about the communication of information, but about evoking a response. The response evoked is not just an intellectual resolve, but is about the commitment of the whole self to a certain way of being and acting. What I am getting at here is that the whole atmosphere of worship is important. This means that the setting, the trappings, the actions, the words are all part of the experience of the worshiper. In my view, worship is an aesthetic experience, and worship that uses its resources to the fullest provides beauty as well as telling the truth and inculcating moral goodness.

By beauty I mean that which evokes satisfaction in all its senses, a balancing of harmony and intensity that allows one to enter into the fullness of life.[9] This means involving as many of the senses as possible. It means care over crafting the words and actions in such a way that chaos and boredom are both avoided. It means providing enough structure that those present feel comfortable and clear about what is happening and what is expected of them, while at the same time leaving room for the unexpected, the grace-filled experience of God.[10] It means providing a setting that allows for one to enter fully into the experience, perhaps through artwork, perhaps through stark simplicity, perhaps through a few symbolic reminders of the kind of experience into which worshipers are being called to enter.

Worship spaces vary enormously from one another, in shape, in size, in simplicity or elaborateness of decor. The spaces reflect both the history of a particular congregation and of a particular denomination. There may be pictorial representations of figures or stories from the Bible or from the tradition. The colors may change with the liturgical season. There may be flowers. There may be symbols. In Protestant churches the Bible is, of course, read, but it is also often found open on the communion table as a symbol of the Word of God become flesh. The Bible is perhaps carried in procession to its place. The empty cross is also commonly found symbolizing the risen Christ. It symbolizes the end of the Christian story, but also, thereby, its entirety. Always there is a table, variously named as communion table, holy table, or altar, depending on how one sees the action that takes place there. At that table, the Eucharist, communion, last supper, sacrifice of the mass is celebrated and enacted. There may be many other symbols, the Greek ιησ or χρ, as shorthand references to Jesus.

The Protestant traditions have often included the singing of congregational hymns (in particular those that appeal to Scripture) and anthems. The act of singing, an act where more than just the word is important, has been one of the most embodied acts in Protestant worship. Some Protestant groups historically worried about the emotions generated by singing and instrumental music. Indeed, if one follows John Wesley's "Directions for Singing," it is definitely an embodied experience: "Sing lustily and with good courage. Beware of singing as if you were half dead or half asleep; but lift up your voice with strength. Be no more afraid of your voice now, nor more ashamed of its being heard, than when you sung the songs of Satan."[11]

Corporate worship has both individual and communal dimensions. Although one comes as an individual, one enters into community. The primary form of Christian worship is communal. The gathering of the people around Jesus becomes the explicit continuation of his community in the world. In worship, one is brought into relationship with God, which, presumably, one could pursue in a solitary and mystical way unconnected to any particular religious tradition. But Christian worship also tells the Christian story. It brings worshipers into relationship with God through Jesus Christ.

Worshipers are also brought into relationship with others. Through participation, congregational identity as Christians is constituted and consolidated. By participating in worship, congregational members are accepting and entering into the Christian way, an acceptance that, ideally, informs action in the world. We are also forging ties with others who have chosen that way, ties that make us a community, a group for which we have some responsibility. We are forging bonds that strengthen and empower us for common life and activity. "Ritual intentionally alters the usual social arrangements and allows the envisioning of a different state of being (communitas)."[12]

In a very real sense the worship space is a microcosm of the whole world. We symbolically name the directions of the four sides of the church with the four points of the compass, the altar or table always being the East. Insofar as the worshiping community is a microcosm of the world, our responsibility is extended far beyond the walls of the worship space.

The forms and words of Christian worship vary greatly from denomination to denomination and congregation to congregation.

In some settings, the same, or virtually the same, words and actions
are used over and over again. Other settings allow for more fluidity
of practice. There is always something repetitive about Christian
worship. Partly this is to conquer the chaos mentioned above. Partly
it is to compress the story and symbols into a manageable form.
Partly it is to provide and forge identity. But Christian worship
develops and changes over time. The history of Christian worship
is not the history of static repetition. Mere repetition is not the sub-
stance of ritual, but of compulsion.

Problems with Christian Worship

If so many are looking for rituals, and if one of the main tools
Christian churches have is access to ritual through worship, why
are Christian churches not full? What is missing in Christian worship that so many appear not to find what they are seeking? How
does Christian worship impede flourishing and right relation?

Christian worship is almost as varied as Christian proclamation,
so my remarks here will be generalizations that do not fit all situations. But when asked to give advice to people who are looking for
places of worship, I find that there are few places that I can actually
recommend.

To some of its detractors, Christian worship seems like magic,
like the manipulation of words and objects by specific actors in a
very stylized and particular way so as to bring about a predictable
result. Certain forms of Christian worship lend themselves more to
this observation than others. But whenever the words, or the actors,
or the forms are so rigid that their ability to be efficacious is compromised by "getting something wrong," then the possibility of
interpreting the rite as "magical" exists. There is no openness to the
divine or to one another in such worship.

One of the main problems with Christian worship is the question of who gets to participate and how. Is there any interchange-
ability of performers, or are the main performers always the same?
Are they always men? What roles do those who are not in the main
performance roles play? Do they sit silently? Do they speak or sing
often, sometimes, or rarely? Do they have a chance to be drawn in
to what is happening? Are there other participative moments and
actions? If the actors are always male, and further, always ordained

males, then they are not representative of the congregation. If the congregation rarely gets to do anything beyond listen, then rather than being participants in the ritual they are observers. Observation does not necessarily draw one in to what is happening. It does not usually lead to as much involvement or commitment as does having a direct role to perform. I do not think it an accident that my own involvement in the church came about through my direct participation in the music life of my childhood congregation. I think it bears reflection that many of those involved in the "new age" movement are seeking rituals in which they are direct or primary actors.

Some theorists argue that ritual simply communicates given power relations to the worshipers who are present to have those relations embodied for them to internalize. Ritual does embody power. When one attends a service of Christian worship, if one is thoughtful, one can see the power relationships at work.[13] One can see how the main actors, the chosen practices, and the process of traditions conspire to give power to those in control of the ritual, a power that often extends far beyond the ritual itself. Catherine Bell argues, however, that ritual is not just a matter of domination, but that ritual involves negotiation with the participants that empowers them as worshipers.[14] In ritual, one comes to appropriate for oneself "definitions of power, personhood and the capacity to act."[15] Ritual, for Bell, allows for the fluidity and interpretation of power relationships. Although one consents by being present, one also resists by not accepting everything as presented, but by appropriating it for oneself.

Does Christian ritual facilitate one's access to the divine, or does it impede that access by positing official actors between the individual worshiper and God? Are the main actors presented as essential to the divine-human relationship? Are they presented *in persona dei* or *in persona Christi* in such a way as to imply that there is no access except through the actor? If one is never given direct access to God but must always approach God through the religious functionary, then this becomes problematic to anyone who rejects the notion that some people are, by virtue of "God-given" or church-given office, of higher and "holier" status than others. It also, in my view, comes close to idolatry to claim that any one category of persons (e.g., ordained men) is more suitable to function as a representative of God or Christ than another. There is a vast difference between seeing ritual as an access to God that one would not be able to have otherwise and seeing ritual as the focused attention on a relationship to God that is possible always and everywhere.

Ritual is problematic if it does not take the community into account. Worship that seems like an interaction only between the main actors and God is a performance for other participants to look at rather than an experience into which they themselves are drawn to participate.

How much space for negotiation is truly communicated in ritual? Even if Bell is correct that there is room for negotiating a relationship to the power and authority as presented, the presentation of that power and authority can take on different tones or modes. The space for negotiation can be presented as open or closed. We will return to this in the next section of this chapter.

How accessible are some of the main stories and symbols being ritualized, and which stories and symbols are emphasized? The waters of baptism are said to represent a variety of meanings of baptism, such as union with Jesus Christ, incorporation into the church, new birth, forgiveness of sin, reception of the Holy Spirit.[16] If the emphasis falls primarily on cleansing from original sin, the result may be a tone and an act that emphasizes the wickedness of humanity and the wrath of God. If this happens, the grace of God in this act may be downplayed or overlooked. I am not saying that the church should minimize sin, but I am saying that if one of the main times we hear about sin is in the context of the baptism of infants, then the story as good news might be lost on many. Given that baptism offers ample possibility to emphasize the gracious love of God surrounding us from our beginnings, the image of God's grace and love should abound.

The bread and wine of the Eucharist represent the body and blood of Jesus Christ. Usually here we have these symbols not simply as representative of Jesus' presence, but being placed in some context of bloody sacrifice, they embody theories of atonement that depend on death for their meaning. The symbol of cross or crucifix is one in which an instrument of torture becomes a central Christian symbol.

I find both the cross and the emphasis on the body and blood of the Eucharist very mixed symbols. In my view, they cannot simply be left to stand uninterpreted as they often have. The cross, empty or as a crucifix, is a powerful symbol of suffering. The cross is an instrument of torture. It is, of course, a point of memory. In seeing the cross we recall, presumably, not just the piece of the story that is the crucifixion, but the story as a whole. Many wear the cross as a sign of their Christian identity. But as a symbol that often stands by itself, it is ambiguous. One looking on the cross might wonder if Christianity can be summed up best through suffering. One might wonder if one is meant not only to recall the suffering of Jesus, but to follow in that suffering way oneself. One might wonder if suffering is somehow the ideal state to be imitated.

Why this symbol and not the empty tomb or loaves and fishes? The empty cross is often seen to symbolize resurrection, but still the symbol remains. Although I do not think that one can change the symbol overnight to another symbol more representative of life than of death, I myself find the symbol of the cross profoundly disturbing. Sometimes it is not a bad thing to be disturbed, to be reminded of the violence in which we live our lives. But as a symbol, the cross must be used carefully, not cavalierly.

With regard to the Eucharist, it seems to me that the sacrificial aspect of the celebration is only one of many, and one that does not have equal standing in all denominations. There is something profound about the recognition of embodiment that is signaled by the symbols of bread and wine, representing body and blood. By themselves, body and blood are the matter of life. Bread and wine represent the food of life. In this case it seems to me that the notion of Jesus' real presence in the Eucharist does not have to be dispensed with in order to get away from the death-dealing symbolism of the broken body and shed blood of human sacrifice. One can recognize the gift of another, the gift of Jesus, in the symbols without necessarily implying that the death of one, even of him, is somehow God's will in order to allow for God's love and salvation.

The problem arises when broken body and the shedding of blood are somehow portrayed as sacrifice to God or satisfaction of God. The recognition of terrible and terrifying death is not the same as the lauding of it. Again, if flourishing and right relationship are to prevail, especially for those who have sacrificed much on the altars of oppression and broken promises, we need to be cognizant of how our eucharistic symbols are presented and interpreted.

Are there ritual openings for those who are appalled by a tradition that seems to depend on blood sacrifice and suffering death? I think there are, but I also think that we have not looked nearly as carefully as we must at what we are communicating in these symbols.

I have resisted seeing Jesus' work as concentrated in his suffering death.[17] Instead, I think we should concentrate on the whole life of Jesus as salvific event. The symbols of eucharist and cross are mixed symbols. They are symbols of the end of Jesus' life that are meant to be understood as abbreviations for the whole. But the abbreviation can get distorted if we do not keep reinterpreting. The bread and wine can be seen as symbols of embodiment rather than as symbols glorifying suffering. The empty cross can be seen as the overcoming of suffering rather than its glorification. These symbols do not have to be the only ones used or emphasized in a ritual that aims for flourishing and right relationship.

Ritual is problematic if not enough care and preparation goes into the planning. If the worship is badly organized or carelessly executed, more chaos is created than is controlled. The expectations of participants are violated, and they cannot enter fully into the experience. Nor are the participants taken seriously as actors if the ritual is careless. Careless ritual implies a lack of importance of the task, of those present, and of the divine. Careless ritual also flies in the face of beauty. If beauty is a balance of harmony and intensity, then a ritual that is too chaotic is not as beautiful as it could be; it does not create the experience of beauty both for the participants and for God. Nor does it create the possibility of opening the worshipers to the experience of transcendence, for structure is needed if the inbreaking of grace/antistructure is to occur and to be recognized and experienced as God.[18]

Ritual also becomes problematic for many when there is no connection to life beyond the ritual. Unless the ritual is related to the ongoing lives of the participants in meaningful ways, it lacks any relevance beyond itself. Ritual can show total disregard for the life choices of those who are present; it can simplify life in terms of moral choices in such a way that participants are unable to make a connection between the worship and the lives they lead. For example, prayers that extol the virtues of family life without an inkling that not everyone lives in the perfect family, free from violence, mental illness, and so on, present a moral picture of a world in which few live.

Worship can also portray and enact the divine-creaturely relationship in less-than-adequate ways, creating rather than solving deep intellectual and theological conundrums. Prayers implying the concern of God primarily for humanity and only secondarily for the rest of creation present a particular picture that one may not want to defend theologically. Liturgies may reinscribe particular views of God's nature, power, and activity that one may not be theologically prepared to defend. The view of God's power that I presented earlier is not, for example, consonant with hymns or prayers that profess God's control of everything.

What Could Good Ritual Do?

By being more than words and by involving more than the intellect, worship gives a value to embodiment. That value is inherent in the experience even though the full weight of that value may be countered in part by other elements of the experience.

Victor Turner speaks of ritual as "liminal."[19] Ritual is time set apart from ordinary time and place set apart from ordinary place. In ritual, one is in a boundary space, a brief hiatus in ordinary life. One is also in a boundary space between the here and now and the transcendent. In Christian worship, the worshipers are removed, however briefly, from their day-to-day lives in such a way that there is space and time for transformation, for something new to happen. This something new, in Christian terms, is the experience of God's grace, God's boundless love.

In worship, one can be given a glimpse of the possible. If the world presented in ritual is not simply mirrored as it is, but as it could be, then worship can foster hope for something different. If this hope is presented as the possibility of flourishing and right relationship, ritual can be an instrument to foster these states of affairs. In worship, care needs to be taken not merely to mirror the values of the community, but to hold open the possibility of genuine change. If the ideal presented or the hope upheld comes only in one idealized and universalizing model, flourishing and right relationship might not be fostered. To use certain family values as an example, again, if the only model of right relationship is one particular kind of family, say two parents and children, then this leaves the possibilities of flourishing out for many who not only do not but never will fit this model.

Unless the primary actors in ritual are drawn from a wide range of identities, life situations, and contexts, the transforming possibilities of ritual are limited by the reinforcement of certain power relationships. Unless, for example, women (including lesbian women) and children, all persons of color, and gay men can be primary actors in Christian worship, the picture of relationship reinforced by the actors themselves can stifle the possibility of right relationship and flourishing. In order to present the broadest possibilities for flourishing, ritual actors need to be as diverse as the community itself desires to be. Right relationship as idealized ought also to be embodied in the actors.

Although I think that Bell is right to see participants in ritual as those who have to negotiate their own relationships vis-à-vis the structure of power as presented in the ritual, the ritual itself should also seek to present the best of the tradition in such a way that the possibilities for flourishing and right relation are more transparent than hidden. This means balancing the historical with the contemporary and presenting the best available theology, both in word and act. The God presented, the God whose presence is requested, must be consonant with the view of God theologically espoused. This means, for instance, that there is no room for simply spouting phrases from the tradition whose theology one would not affirm or enacting a God of coercion and wrath in sacrament or symbol.

The affirmation of embodiment is more fully enacted when participants as well as main actors get to act. This does not necessarily mean that everyone does everything, but it does mean that no one is a spectator. Everyone ought to be invited into some full-bodied participation, whether in singing, or in speaking, or in movement.

Worship gives participants a chance to be involved in the creation of beauty while still keeping chaos at bay and portraying the order and relations of the universe. Good worship always seeks a balance between harmony and intensity. If worship is too comfortable, too trite, there is neither challenge to growth nor opening for grace. If worship is too unpredictable, too confusing, the opening for grace is again lost as participants scramble to keep up.

Christian worship is a communal act. What takes place is not just between an individual and the God of Jesus Christ. Worship brings together a diverse group and, through shared word and symbol, opens the possibility of community, not just community in worship, but communal identity beyond. Belonging to a community is a matter of give and take. One accepts one's identity as part of the community, but one may also be actively working to be part of forging growth or change in that identity. In a community one says "these are my people." But this does not necessarily mean total identification of self with the community and what it stands for.

In worship one does not have to agree with or directly participate in absolutely everything that happens to affirm one's sense of belonging. But unless there are some important connections, the identity of the community ceases to be important to the identity of the individual. If I can no longer say the words with integrity, if I cannot act in concert with the group, I may no longer be able to belong there.

Conversely, if I can participate with integrity, I may well be drawn beyond myself into a whole that can be greater than the sum of its parts. I affirm my own identity as a social being connected to the universe in myriad ways. I understand myself as interrelated. I participate in some of those connections.

What would make for Christian worship that promotes right relationship and flourishing? The words and symbols need to point to life, life in all its ambiguities. They need to point to the hope that flourishing and right relationship could be possible without denying the very real challenges to that flourishing and right relationship. The words need to be inclusive, and the practices need to give a wide variety of actors exposure. In addition, the whole community needs to be involved in participating rather than in being spectators. The God addressed needs to be the God affirmed, a God who desires life and not death, for whom flourishing and right relation is important. The Jesus Christ re-presented in word and sacrament needs to be the one who calls to fullness of life. The possibility of relationship to God, to Jesus, and to one another would be open and inviting. I am not here advocating that challenge and judgment do not belong in worship. Far from it. But the challenges must be contextually relevant to the hearers. And the judgment proclaimed must be consonant with the gospel, not just a reinscription of the power and authority of the human actors.

Worship presented as a closed, hermetically sealed whole leaves no room for the struggle that characterizes the Christian life. It leaves no openings for grace. It leaves no possibilities for transformation. It leaves no spaces for the truly human and the truly divine to meet and relate.

Yet the possibilities for worship are enormous. Worship allows for the involvement of the whole human being in human community with the divine. It requires intellectual, moral, and aesthetic commitment.

Sample Eucharistic Prayer

As a way to focus thought on some of the issues raised in this chapter, I provide a sample prayer that provides some words and images as one example of how one can begin the process of a ritual that fosters flourishing and right relationship. The words and images are, of course, selective, but seek to provide openings for grace.

Prayer:

Lift up your hearts!

We lift them up to God!

Let us give thanks to our gracious God.

It is right to give God thanks and praise.

God, Creator of all and Provider for all,
    we give you thanks and praise.
You brought forth the first humans from the earth and
    from the beginning set them in a garden of plenty.
You provided water and manna and quails
    to those wandering in the wilderness.
You gave oil and meal to the widow of Zarephath.
You continue to nurture us at your breast
    and fold us under your wings.

Holy, Holy, Holy Lord,
    God of power and might,
    heaven and earth are full of your glory.
Hosanna in the highest.
Blessed is the one who comes in the name of the Lord.
Hosanna in the highest.

We give you thanks, O God,
    for the gift of Jesus,
    the bread of life and the true vine.
He came among us as one who shared the banquet
    of your grace with all.

He feasted with those who had never been full.
He brought to his table those who had been outcast.
In the simplest meal of loaves and fish,
    bodies and spirits were fed.

As Jesus and his followers shared one last meal together,
    he took bread, gave thanks to you, broke the bread,
    and gave it to his disciples, saying:
    "This is my body that is for you.
    Do this in remembrance of me."
After they had finished eating, he took the cup,
    gave thanks to you,
    and gave it to his disciples, saying:
    "This cup is the new covenant in my blood.
    Do this, as often as you drink it, in remembrance of me."

You, O God, who fill our hungry souls and bodies with food,
    come now to us gathered at this table.
Send your Holy Spirit among us, and upon these gifts,
    that the simple foods of bread and wine,
    given to nourish our hunger, may be for us
    communion in the body and blood of Jesus Christ.

Companion God, who joins us in the breaking of bread,
    may we who are filled share our bounty with others
    until we all feast together in the heavenly banquet.

Through Jesus Christ, Sophia embodied for us,
    with the Holy Spirit, Sophia present to us,
    all honor and glory is yours, Sophia our Mother,
    now and forever.

And now with the confidence of the children of God, we say . . .

The Lord's Prayer

Invitation to the Table:

Wisdom has built her house, she has hewn seven pillars.
She has prepared the meal;

she has set her table and sent out her servants.
She calls from the highest places in the town:
"Come, eat of my bread and drink of the wine I have mixed.
Lay aside immaturity and live; walk in the way of insight."

Fraction

Serving of Communion

Prayer After Communion (in unison):

**God, our Creator, you give us a share in the one bread and
the one cup, and make us one in Christ. Help us to bring
your salvation and joy to all the world. Amen**

NOTES

1. James F. White, *Introduction to Christian Worship*, revised edition (Nashville: Abingdon, 1990), 23–24.

2. John Calvin, *Institutes of the Christian Religion*, edited by John T. McNeill, translated and indexed by Ford Lewis Battles (Philadelphia: Westminster, 1977), 2, 1279.

3. See, for example, Catherine Bell, *Ritual Theory, Ritual Practice* (New York: Oxford, 1992); Catherine Bell, *Ritual: Perspectives and Dimensions* (New York: Oxford, 1997); Ronald L. Grimes, *Beginnings in Ritual Studies* (Lanham, N.Y.: University Press of America, 1982); Ronald L. Grimes, *Ritual Criticism* (Columbia, S.C.: University of South Carolina Press, 1990); Victor Turner, ed., *Celebration: Studies in Festivity and Ritual* (Washington, D.C.: Smithsonian Institution Press, 1982).

4. Bell, *Ritual*, x.

5. Ibid., xi.

6. White, *Introduction to Christian Worship*, 29–30.

7. See, for example, Turner, "Introduction," in Turner, ed., *Celebration*, 29.

8. Sylvia Dunstan, "Crashing Waters at Creation," found in

Voices United: The Hymn and Worship Book of The United Church of Canada (Toronto: The United Church Publishing House, 1996), 449.

9. See my *Christ in a Post-Christian World: How Can We Believe in Jesus Christ When Those Around Us Believe Differently—or Not at All?* (Minneapolis: Fortress, 1995).

10. Carol Doran and Thomas H. Troeger, *Trouble at the Table: Gathering the Tribes for Worship* (Nashville: Abingdon, 1996), 94–100. Doran and Troeger call these poles structure and anti-structure.

11. John Wesley, *Select Hymns*, 1761.

12. Nancy Tatom Ammerman, with Arthur E. Farnsley II et al., *Congregation and Community* (New Brunswick: Rutgers University Press, 1997), 369.

13. Bell, *Ritual Theory, Ritual Practice*, 206.

14. Ibid., 211.

15. Ibid., 218.

16. White, *Introduction to Christian Worship*, 208–209.

17. See my "Beyond Moral Influence to An Atoning Life," *Theology Today* 52 (1995): 344–55.

18. Doran and Troeger, *Trouble at the Table*, 94–100.

19. See, for example, Turner, "Introduction," in Turner, ed., *Celebration*, 29.

8. Life Inside and Outside the Congregation

Community and Personal Formation

Although a sense of liberal individualism that posits the isolated individual standing outside and apart from whatever he or she is viewing is pervasive in today's North America, there are many reasons to call this view of humanity into question.[1] Feminists and others have pointed out that the freedoms that one has to make choices are bounded by one's gender, geography, ethnic origin, class, and so on. There is no "level playing field" of isolated individuals. In economic terms, even in Canada, where the "social safety net" has historically been prized, the prevailing economics is about taking care of oneself first. Further, critics of this view have noticed that the questions we learn to ask and the answers we view as acceptable to those questions are profoundly influenced by the various dimensions of our contexts. It is not that we cannot see beyond the most narrow of perspectives (see my argument about transcendence above), but it is the case that our contextual realities make a difference to what we see and how we see it.

Because we recognize the voluntary dimension of identifying with many of our historically given communities, belonging to something is not necessarily a given. Whereas at one time more of us would have belonged to religious institutions, had a sense of belonging to and with the geographical community in which we lived, even had a sense of school pride, now many of us have no sense of belonging or a very different sense of belonging than we once had.[2] Now communities of affiliation are choices that we must consciously make. Yet, despite the common view that we are isolated individuals, many people seem to be searching for a sense of belonging. We long for a group of people with whom we can be ourselves, where our sense of alienation from self and others is overcome, and where self-sufficiency is exposed as only one (albeit pervasive) view of the ideal individual. Many of us long to be part of something bigger than ourselves, even though we know that the downside of such belonging may be in part to compromise or restrain individual identity for a sense of the group's identity. Yet also, for many of us, especially those who have historically been denied the autonomy of the liberal ideal, there are things we cannot or are not willing to give up, even for that goal of belonging. Maintaining a strong sense of self is crucial for our own sense of well-being in the world. Yet we also ask, What groups of people can we identify ourselves with sufficiently that we can name ourselves as belonging to those groups? And we may belong to several groups at the same time rather than relying on one group for our whole sense of identity.

Belonging to a Christian church—that is, to a particular congregation—is one way to belong to a community. Here I am suggesting that one of the resources that churches have for promoting flourishing and right relationship is precisely that they provide communities of affiliation. Not all church communities provide flourishing and right relationship for all those within their bounds. Indeed, as I noted earlier, sometimes the church has been seen to cut off flourishing and right relationship for some of its members. What I want to do in this chapter is to explore how the congregation as community might be a resource rather than a hindrance for flourishing and right relationship; how the congregation might— precisely through being a community or even several communities, thereby providing a sense a belonging—embody God's transforming grace. Here I am mostly concentrating on individual congregations as venues of community, although most gain part of their identity from their denominational affiliation and have within them many smaller groups or communities.

In her book *Coming Together/Coming Apart: Religion, Community and Modernity*, Elizabeth Bounds suggests some common uses of "community."

> Sifting through the variety of uses for the concept of community, I find a few related, yet distinct meanings:

1. a desire for "immediate relations," an arena of meaningful love and solidarity and/or spirituality, in contrast to reified social roles;

2. a desire for collective connection (often rooted in ethnic and racial heritage) in reaction to what is perceived as a dangerous, conflicted and/or confusing pluralized society;

3. a desire for the experience of a unified transcendence, a meaningful whole, so that life is lived in relation to something *greater* than the self (often expressed in religious or nationalist language);

4. a desire to reaffirm a lost or eroded set of traditions and practices;

5. a desire to create a new set of practices in the face of a society that denies or negates the existence of one's self and one's group;

6. a desire for effective political participation, seeing oneself as a citizen among fellow citizens with relations and responsibilities.[3]

The communities desired or envisaged in each of these options vary, and not all are mutually compatible. Various churches and congregations have provided and continue to provide a venue for each of these desires at varying times and places. Here I will examine each briefly in light of the vision of church presented in this book. I will examine the goals of flourishing and right relationship that I have named to see if these different possibilities shed light on ways to talk about the community offered by churches and thus ways congregations might begin to think of themselves. A congregation also might adopt a number of these desiderata simultaneously, but may see some as central or uncompromisable and others as peripheral.

In turn-of-the-millennium North America, churches are voluntary organizations. Church membership in once-mainline churches is on the decline. If Christians see themselves and their way of life as threatened by "secular" society, they might well adopt as their self-chosen ideal numbers 2 ("a desire for collective connection . . . in reaction to what is perceived as dangerous, conflicted and/or confusing pluralized society") and/or 4 ("a desire to reaffirm a lost or eroded set of traditions and practices") above. In number 2, churches function as the arbiter of truth and values in the face of a

society that offers too many choices. One sure place remains. In
such a view of church, maintaining communal identification over
individuality is paramount to keeping the boundaries clear. It
would be possible to see those inside as more worthy of concern
than the vast world outside. If too much variation is allowed, the
congregation becomes like the society it is seeking respite from. In
such a community, diversity is not privileged. Change is not welcomed, for the community's identity and security rests on being certain of itself. Challenge is not tolerated. Although one can see that
there might be good reasons for communities, perhaps especially
communities rooted in nondominant ethnic or racial heritage, to
want to preserve identity in light of their marginalization by the dominant group(s) or out of desire not to succumb to the homogenizing
effects of North American culture, the dangers of such identification
must be kept in mind if flourishing and right relation for all of creation is the goal. Of course, there may well be congregations that
gather along ethnic or racial lines where the identity is not fostered or
enforced by a reactionary desire to filter out other influences.

In adopting number 4 ("a desire to reaffirm a lost or eroded set
of traditions and practices") as a desideratum, history becomes crucial. But the use to which history is put could vary. A church community could reaffirm its historical beliefs and practices as a way to
challenge the present, or it could reaffirm its history as a way to
escape the present. As I have made clear in my vision of churches,
history is a constituting factor; indeed, the "shared memory . . . of
Jesus Christ" is a large part of what identifies churches as Christian.
Yet, uncritically adopted, the history of the church, which is always
a partial and interpreted history, can foster and has fostered lack of
grace for many. If one is to reaffirm traditions and practices, that
must be critically done with an eye on their present validity and usefulness for flourishing and right relation.

The first ideal, a desire for "an arena of meaningful love and solidarity and/or spirituality, in contrast to reified social roles," suggests
sufficient homogeneity that one can identify with the goals of the
community, in contrast, perhaps even as a challenge, to those that
society seems to give as status quo. Here the congregation challenges the dominant culture by providing a place to give and
receive love, acceptance, and spiritual nurture with those who have
a similar worldview. Here again one has to ask how much homogeneity is imposed by this community and whether the contrast to

the social roles of the status quo is a challenge that fosters or impedes flourishing and right relationship.

However else one might perceive or present the congregation, it is a community that agrees, at least in its broadest terms, on its aim to provide or focus "the experience of a unified transcendence . . . so that life is lived in relation to something *greater* than the self" (number 3). There may be a great deal of debate about how properly or most adequately to conceive of God. There may even be debate about whether traditional notions of transcendence should be used; but in the terms in which transcendence is defined in this book, God provides that unified transcendence to which Christians appeal. One can also include in transcendence shared ideals such as flourishing and right relationship, which are greater than individual selves alone can bring about, and around which communities can make common cause.

A congregation may also want to present itself as a community that creates "a new set of practices in the face of a society that denies or negates the existence of one's self and one's group" (number 5). That is, congregations may be looking for new practices that stand alongside or replace older practices in order to affirm the group as a specific community of Christians (e.g., women or a racial or ethnic minority) that has historically not been taken seriously in the practices of the church. This meaning of community recognizes and privileges diversity and the possibility that not all congregations or Christians are necessarily the very same. If the community truly wants to understand and eradicate historical and systemic oppressions, it needs to listen to, learn from, and live from the experiences of those who have been oppressed. This may mean that not all experiences are given equal privilege, for the community may need to learn more from the experiences of some so it can foster flourishing and right relationship for all.

A church may see itself as a vehicle for effective political participation, within its own practices, policy making, and so on, and in relation to the wider society of which it is a part (number 6). In this final view of community presented by Bounds, the diversity of community is recognized as the right and responsibility of all members to participate in it.

From Bounds' discussion of community it is clear that communities themselves must make some decisions about who they are and about how they should present themselves to the world. This presentation might take place explicitly as a congregation defines itself in a publicly accessible way, or implicitly, where the identity of the congregation can be known only by observation or participation. Out of this discussion we can perhaps pull together some pointers about how a congregation might want to view and present itself as a vehicle for community if it seeks to understand itself according to the definition presented in this book.

Bounds' various views of community make us conscious of the question of homogeneity and diversity. Some denominations and some congregations have views of right belief and practice that make it difficult for members to raise new issues or question old practices. The view of churches that I have presented in this book is one that tries to see churches as bounded, but with permeable boundaries. The vision of churches that I have presented does not have rigidly orthodox views of belief systems; there is no list of "fundamentals." Yet churches do have an identity that is taken from Jesus Christ, even though, admittedly, taken from Jesus Christ as interpreted by this particular theologian in a particular time and place. The vision of churches presented here does not presume that individuals or congregations would face a "test" of whether they should be in or out, but, rather, that it makes little sense to affiliate oneself with the Christian church unless one wants to belong to a community with Jesus at its center. Here I envisage that within this identity, much diversity would be not just tolerated, but welcomed. Further, individual congregations can hone that identity to suit the times and places in which they find themselves, so long as they do not use their beliefs as a weapon to exclude those who do not conform.

The same would hold true for diversity of practice. Here, the boundary is the issue of whether a practice fosters or impedes flourishing and right relationship. In the case of both belief and relationship, the kind of community that is envisaged in this definition is one where there is vigorous debate about options and tolerance of difference when no agreement is possible. I hasten to assert that I do not envisage a community where "anything goes," but I do envisage a community where the voluntary nature of participation is taken seriously. That is, given what the community stands for, people need to make their own choices about opting in or out. Such a community is very different from one that would welcome continued participation only if questioning is bracketed.

The congregation as defined here would offer "an arena of meaningful love and solidarity and/or spirituality, in contrast to reified social roles" (number 1) if it challenged the status quo in the name of flourishing and right relationship for all. Thus the church needs to see itself partly as a "community of resistance," a challenge to the rest of the social world if the social world beyond the church is not itself fostering flourishing and right relationship.[4] As here envisaged, the congregation would be a safe space where one could be nurtured and given support to challenge beliefs and practices that compromise the full humanity of its members. Such a church community would also recognize that class, ethnic or geographic origin, sexual orientation, and so on, might mean that various members and adherents experience the possibilities for flourishing and right relationship differently. Those who are differently (and more) privileged by society beyond the church would be part of challenging that privilege on behalf of others in their midst, both internally to the congregation and externally to the world beyond it. (For the more specific roles of preaching, teaching, and ritual, see chapters 6 and 7.)

The permeable boundaries of the congregation also mean that it cannot and should not cut itself off from meaningful relationship to those who do not consider themselves part of a church. The churches' arena of concern is the whole of creation. These permeable boundaries also mean that a congregation cannot concern itself only with things defined as "spiritual," if spiritual is separated from embodiment. Flourishing and right relationship concern whole beings. Therefore, churches need to concern themselves with whole beings.

The churches envisaged in this definition will be communities that respect the diversities of their members and allow for the growth and development of individual selves. This growth and development, however, does not mean privileging the individual over the whole of creation. When my purported flourishing (in terms of acquisition of goods or claiming of rights) comes at the expense of the flourishing of others, right relationship is compromised. Here, of course, vigorous thought and debate are needed about the limits of the individual, for only when multiple voices in the debate are heard can one come to some agreements about where the whole must take priority over one of its individual parts.

In the churches envisaged here, the decision-making processes will be widely representative and give voice to a variety of points of view. This means that no decisions can be taken without diverse input. Any institution, such as a church, as part of the context in which we are formed and learn to live, has an effect on the persons and the societies we become. Problems arise, in view of the ideal presented here, when formation becomes enforcement that does not allow for challenge. The leadership of a church committed to embodying God's grace for all creation must be widely diverse and open to hearing from its whole constituency. The community that would result from such leadership would be one that is itself brought to flourishing and right relationship while fostering the same for others. Those who are looking for community today but who currently experience themselves as disenfranchised by the church will not be interested in affiliating with a community that will not recognize them as active participants in theological formation, in ritual action, and in decision-making processes.[5]

The church is a ready-made community. It can provide a sense of belonging for those who are looking for others with whom to share important matters of meaning and activities related to living out responses to that meaning. Such belonging is only viable for many North Americans today if it takes account of the complexities of life as lived and the historical character of human thought rather than proclaiming a never-changing message. Such belonging is also viable for many only if belonging to the church does not mean having to devalue other communities of affiliation and if the community's concern for creatures extends beyond its own narrow boundaries.

The church community as I paint it here is a community of struggle, a pilgrim community where fellow travelers can share the journey. Working out right relationship is not necessarily easy or self-evident. Thus the struggle is in figuring out, not just as individuals, but as a corporate body, what the congregation ought to be about and how it should go about acting corporately for the whole of creation. Such struggle involves risk; it involves not knowing exactly what will happen next, but knowing that one must live fully into the future. The community is never static. Time passes; members come and go. The most pressing needs for flourishing and right relationship change around us. The church is on a journey rather than planted firmly in one place. In embodying the transforming grace of God, the church must be a transformed community and a community of transformation.

One of Bounds' ideals of community includes "a desire for . . . an arena of meaningful . . . spirituality" (number 1). Many of today's religious searchers would describe what they are looking for as "spirituality." Earlier in this book, the church's resources of teaching, preaching, ritual, and communal action are treated as resources for spirituality. Here I want to focus on some other ways in which the church community is a resource for nurturing individual and communal religious practice outside formal services of worship.

When people describe what they are looking for as spirituality, often they have in mind individual spiritual practices such as prayer or meditation. I think this notion of individual practice is fostered partly by the individualism of liberalism and partly by the fact that people fear being drawn into an institutional practice that does not meet their specific needs.

On the one hand, the individualism of any such practice can lead to a lack of connectedness to any community that would foster the experience of a "unified transcendence" (number 3). On the other hand, even in an institutionalized community such as a church, room needs to be made for individual as well as corporate practice. For the purpose of this book, I am interested only in forms of "spiritual practice" that take place in the context of the Christian church, that is, practice that is somehow affiliated with the Christian community and sees itself as related to that community. This is not to say that there are not many other valid forms of spiritual practice that might well take their inspiration and forms from elsewhere.

The terms *spiritual* and *spirituality* are problematic for a number of reasons. First, in a view of the church such as the one being portrayed here, embodiment is important. There is no disembodied spirit that one cultivates. Cultivating a Christian life includes the whole human being. Cultivating a Christian life includes much more than cultivating an interior spiritual practice. When some of the Protestant students who are in my classes in theology talk about lack of "spirituality" or "spiritual discipline" in the theological college where I teach, what they mean is lack of a particular sort or set of spiritual practices, usually concentration on one-on-one spiritual direction and prayer. It is difficult to convince them that theological study historically, especially in the Reformed traditions, can be a spiritual discipline, and that social activity on behalf of the poor

can be a spiritual practice.[6] Second, the term *spiritual,* connected
as it is with the Holy Spirit, which "blows where it will," can be used
as a way to avoid accountability to the community out of which the
practice grows. That is, even in individual practice, if one is seeking
a life in Christian community, something that is "good for me"
cannot be the only criterion. If the practice cuts one off from
Christian community or does not have the result of concern for the
whole of creation, including the whole self, then it is not practice
that the churches I have envisaged here should encourage.

Christian practice, whether individual or communal, has as its
purpose the fostering of flourishing and right relationship of a
human self with God, with self, and with the neighbor, human or
otherwise. "Right relationship" reminds us that we live in an interconnected world where my "interior life" is connected intimately
with who I am and how I live, and where who I am and how I live
is connected with the rest of the cosmos. If Christian practice is
understood in this way rather than as my practice for my sake alone,
then the role of various Christian practices at this time in history
becomes clearer.

I do not mean here to discount the need for individual Christian
practitioners to develop a sense of the self through practice. But
solipsism can easily result if we forget that "Who am I?" is only half
the question. The rest of the question is: "in relation to God, my
human neighbor, the whole created world, the dog, the cat, and so
on." Then language of eros points us to the wholeness of relationship and the need to be whole beings in connection with ourselves
and all the myriad others of the world.

Today we mostly think of changed practice following from a
changed attitude; but as Margaret Miles reminds us, "historical
people thought it obvious that insight follows change; changed
behavior—changed activities—*produce* insight."[7] "Practices both
prepare the conditions under which religious experiences are likely
to occur and, subsequent to such experiences, provide a lifestyle
that integrates and perpetuates them."[8] Christian practice that produces a changed self allows for the possibility that this changed self
and its changed view of its relationships might challenge the soci-
etally given status quo. One can see, however, that the fostering of
any practice on the part of a church has the potential to be a two-
edged sword. What could challenge the status quo in one time or
one way might also become an instrument of nonquestioning

socialization in another. This two-edged possibility is the reason that one should never give up a fully critical view of the society of which one is a part, or of any institution, church included, that is part of that society. Nor should one give up the notion of one's own selfhood. Recognition of the profound interconnection of all things does not mean that one has to give up a sense of self. Rather, it means that one needs to develop a critical perspective on one's place within that whole and on one's responsibilities both to the whole and to specific parts, including one's own self.

Prayer and Asceticism

I want to examine briefly two specific practices that have historical weight in Christianity: prayer and asceticism. I also want to look at what the role of "spiritual direction" might be in a turn-of-the-millennium North America Protestant congregation.

The practice of individual prayer, often according to a given pattern, has long been part of the Christian tradition. "Although practices of prayer have taken a variety of forms, prayer, understood most broadly, is a habit of interior attentiveness, an activity that creates a formerly unknown self, a self neither imagined nor sought by secular culture."[9] In relational terms, prayer is bringing oneself into focused relationship with God with a view to being a self more in tune with the will of God.

Individual prayer is sometimes explicitly verbal, sometimes not; sometimes expressed audibly, sometimes not; sometimes expressed according to set forms, sometimes not. Historically, there are discussions of the best times and places for prayer. "In short, ingenuity and self-knowledge have always been required for the discernment of methods of prayer that maximally nourish a religious self!"[10]

In the context of the definition of church with which we are working, prayer can be an important tool for an individual who wants better to discern his or her own place and role in relation to God and others. It can also be an important part of forming a self-identity that need not be the self-identity given by socialization. If a historical set form of prayer is used, perhaps it needs to be balanced with forms that, for instance, give a broader set of images for God or attend to the life and work of Jesus in terms and images beyond the sacrificial. In Ignatian spirituality, for example, there is much

reflection on the image of joining God, the king who seeks to conquer infidels.[11] Thus, one needs to recognize the historical time and
place of the form one is using rather than "turning the form into a
formula."[12] But we also need to develop new forms of prayer that
take the individual's and community's context into account. So we
need forms of prayer that arise out of women's experiences, the
experiences of being part of a racial or ethnic minority, and so on.

Prayer can also be part of forming a self-identity for those who are
not historically expected to enter into self-development. Thus, for
instance, women who have historically been socialized to be self-
effacing may find the practice of prayer useful as one way to
develop a stronger sense of themselves.

Prayer can be part of cultivating who one is and wants to be as a
person through cultivating a sense of self in relation to God and to
the world. It can help us to focus on our own particular roles and
responsibilities in the world. It can give us the time and space to
practice serious discernment about the person we want to be and
need to be as we seek to embody God's grace and foster flourishing
and right relationship.

Prayer can be used narcissistically. As much as any other, it can
be a practice that bolsters pride and provides a means of avoiding
the world around one—"sublime self-intending."[13] When the move
to developing one's "spirituality" through prayer is done at the
expense of recognizing any other part of the Christian life as equally
important, then the Christian life becomes attenuated and separated from life as lived.

Prayer does not need to be just a disembodied activity. In the history of the tradition, times and places and postures for prayer have
been suggested or prescribed. Such attention to time, place, and
posture reminds us that we are not disembodied beings seeking our
true spiritual homes elsewhere than in this flesh. Various aids to
prayer such as symbols or artistic images, candles or music remind
us that we are beings who interact with the world around us in a
variety of sensory ways.

Nor should prayer be separated from and elevated over life lived.
Prayer that understands its role as discernment of place and relationship is prayer that understands that it is not a substitute for life
in the world. Although prayer, like public worship, can be a way to
focus our attention on ourselves in relation to God, our relation to
God is not confined to those focused moments. Prayer is one way

to be nourished for our journey. But if the journey includes all of creation, then we have an obligation to share rather than hoard the experience of grace that prayer can help to foster.

Communities can foster the practice of individual or small-group prayer by providing models or groups. Rather than offering one such model, a variety of models could be provided. People could learn from one another how to balance the individual practice with life in the world. In the once-mainline Protestant churches, we have in recent times spent very little effort on helping people to cultivate a balanced prayer life. We have talked far more about doing than about being. As the ideal of churches that I have here portrayed makes clear, doing is crucial. But churches do not act for their own sake. Their motivation for acting transcends their own existence. In part, the motivation is ultimately transcendent, seeking to embody God's transforming grace. In part, its motivation is transcendent insofar as the sphere of concern is the whole of creation, not just a congregation's own well-being and continued existence. In our market-oriented world of turn-of-the-millennium North America, where being busy is seen as a primary good, perhaps churches should return to more serious endorsement of the practice of prayer as one way to remove us from the treadmill where no time is given or privileged for reflection of any sort. If one's life is all activity and no reflection, one soon loses sight of what aims one is serving and whether one truly wants to live one's life endorsing and fostering those aims.

Historically, ascetic practices have been endorsed by Christians. In the name of taming the body and disciplining the spirit, Christians have fasted, have abstained from sex, and have engaged in other practices that have "mortified the flesh." Much of the practice of asceticism in the history of Christianity has rested on a dualism of flesh and spirit that has seen the flesh as an impediment to the true life of the spirit and has identified women more with flesh, thereby devaluing them. But here I have been arguing for the goodness of bodies and embodiment. Flourishing and right relationship are values that recognize and celebrate embodiment. Thus any suggestion that the body's needs and desires are antithetical to true spirituality is problematic for a nondualistic view of the cosmos, where we are and act precisely as embodied and where we are not seeking to escape our bodies, but to be fully who we are as embodied. One can certainly misuse or abuse one's own body and the bodies of others. But the answer is, then, not to "tame" or deny the body, but to learn to treat bodies lovingly and well so that flourishing and right relationship become more likely. Thus I can see no useful way to reclaim the tradition of asceticism as useful in a community of eros.

Spiritual Direction

I am somewhat wary of the term *spiritual direction* because it might be seen to imply (and certainly has in the church sometimes taken the form of) someone else telling an individual how to go about developing his or her own spiritual life. Yet encouragement for the cultivation of relationships of self, God, and the other which require a disciplined focus and specific attention, is a resource that the church can offer. What forms would such an offering take in the church as community of eros? Different people's needs are met in different ways even by the same church congregation. But what churches can do is to make it clear that they have concerns about whole persons, their material needs and their needs for development of relationships of transcendence. In Protestant churches we can begin again to talk and encourage discussion specifically about what it means to cultivate a relationship with God and what sort of self and community develops from that relationship. This is not so we can become "spiritual," as if all the other things one does in practicing the Christian life are not "spiritual." Rather, it is to cultivate one more dimension of what it means to be human, and thus to live fully in flourishing and right relationship.

I have been struck by how comfortable we are in my own denomination, The United Church of Canada, discussing social activism as a sine qua non of Christian living, yet we have not traditionally given as much focus to prayer and Bible study groups. Partly, I think, this is because we live in a culture where doing is far more prized than being, where activity is everything. Partly, I think, it is because we have assumed that individual prayer and meditation will take care of itself (perhaps it did more at one time in Protestantism than it does now). We often do not put nearly as much conscious energy into encouraging lives that include contemplation or silence, one of the results being that our church lives are often like our work lives, too full for attending to the unexpected.

Churches could encourage the practice of silence and listening. They could encourage attentiveness to what is happening in our various relationships. They could be open to the possibilities that once frenetic activity stops one may find oneself in the face of the startling and unforeseen. One of the hardest lessons I had to learn when I was a new teacher was to leave room in the class for the unanticipated. I was so afraid that the students would think I did not know what I was teaching if I couldn't anticipate every bit of learning that might take place. But when I learned to leave some space in class outlines for students to present topics to the class that were their central concern rather than topics I had predetermined, I discovered that the learning experience was enriched for everyone, including me.

I think our lives are a lot like the classroom process. Sometimes we have to learn to give up a bit of control so that novelty can open us to greater flourishing and more possibilities of right relationship. Church communities could help us to learn to attend to God, ourselves, and one another by providing time and space for silence as well as for speech—and time and space for sharing the experiences found in that silence. Congregations are already gathered groups of people where, if the boundaries are truly permeable, they afford space and welcome to find one's place both within the group and within the larger whole of the universe.

Congregational Definition

One of the ways in which a congregation declares who it is to the rest of the world is through developing some kind of statement about congregational identity. My own congregation developed such a statement a couple of years ago. I share it here as one example.

A Vision Statement of Chalmers United Church[14]

Chalmers is a community of God's people who embrace Christian tradition and encourage new ideas.

We gather to:
  Celebrate God's love;

Search and be challenged;
Nurture and be nurtured.

We seek to:
Welcome all who come;
Engage all ages in ministry;
Be guided by faith in daily life; and
Be a compassionate, hopeful presence in the world.

We are not alone. Thanks be to God!

The congregation arrived at this statement through a series of
small-group and congregational meetings where everyone had the
opportunity to participate. The statement reflects the church's
United Church of Canada identity by echoing the New Creed of
the United Church, first adopted in 1968 and revised in the 1980s.
For example, the final line is a direct quote from the creed, and
other lines echo the style and content.

The church's sense of itself as historical is seen as the "Christian
tradition" is affirmed, but the statement also signals that "new ideas,
searching, and challenge are welcome." The congregation also
wants to make it clear that all are welcome. The small group in
which I participated when this statement was in its formative phases
discussed how to name that welcome. Should we, for instance,
name racial identity or sexual orientation specifically? In the end,
age was the only named diversity, but others were clearly in mind.
The congregation wanted to signal that its vision extended beyond
itself to the world, but it also wanted to signal that it wanted to be a
place to nurture people in the Christian faith.

I do not presume that any congregation ever fully lives up to its
own vision of itself, but I think it is important that a congregation
have such a vision, both as a way to keep itself accountable and as
a way to present itself to the world beyond its doors.

Action

If churches are to foster flourishing and right relationship, not just
within their own walls but beyond them—for all creation—then as
institutions, as congregations, and as individuals our activity needs

to attend to these goals. Churches ought to be instruments of social transformation. One of the resources that churches have to keep themselves from being irrelevant in this turn-of-the-millennium world is that they are well positioned to be a force for social transformation. By social transformation I mean seeking actively to change the world from a place that impedes flourishing and right relationship to a place that fosters these values.

The congregation offers a base for social action. There is a critical mass of people with whom one can work. And it offers a motivation for social action. One acts in accordance with the imperatives suggested by the gospel message. Congregations are existing communities; therefore there is already a possibility of like-minded others with whom one can act. One does not have to go searching for a community of interest; one already has that in the church. The possibility of like-mindedness is not the guarantee of like-mindedness. But the shared memory and presence of Jesus Christ and the desire to enact God's transforming grace do at least offer some concrete starting points in terms of discussion about the methods and forms of social action in which the church can and should be engaged.

Although throughout history churches have always seen themselves as having a mission to those less fortunate, the form that the imperative has taken has not always been the form of social transformation. For much of its history and in many geographical places, churches have been content to act mostly in ways that might be called "charity" to the neighbor. By charity here I mean acting in ways that alleviate immediate needs as they present themselves without necessarily asking broader and more systemic questions about whether one should seek to alleviate the ongoing causes of those needs. One might, for example, feed a hungry person who comes to the door or give money to a cause that will feed people in a famine. This important task of keeping one or a few people from suffering ought not be denigrated. But unless one also asks whether there are ways to keep these people from starving in the future, one has not undertaken the task of social transformation as I envisage it here.

Sometimes Christians have decided not to involve themselves in transforming the world because they have thought that God is in control of history and therefore what happens is God's will. Sometimes they have argued that spirituality and politics do not mix and that those who are intent on the "spiritual" should not contaminate

themselves with the "political." Sometimes they have argued that
Jesus did not seem to have a political-social plan for the reformation
of society; therefore, in following Jesus' example, one does specific
works of charity but one does not enter into the political fray of
changing systems.

In the model of church presented here, however, political and
social action is expected as part of the Christian life and the life of
a church. Once we have come to historical consciousness, we see
that the society in which we live is humanly constructed and can be
humanly changed. Since the Enlightenment we have come to realize that many of the forces we once assumed as divine or as fate are
complex systems of social and political and economic interrelating
that have been made by humans. We see it in revolutions and
movements for democracy. The human construction of social systems has been acknowledged in theology by such movements as the
social gospel movement at the turn of the past century and, more
recently, by liberation theologies of a wide variety of types. Although,
for example, some have appealed (and still do appeal) to seeing the
subordination of females to males as God's will, if we are attentive to
the forces that have shaped past and present, we can see that the way
women and men relate to one another is, at least in large measure,
a historical construction that could be changed by human will and
action. Certainly the value society accords each sex in that relating
is humanly accorded, not divinely inspired. Once we know that our
social and cultural systems can be changed, we cannot avoid the
question of our responsibility for how things are and for making
things different from how they are. If part of the brunt of poverty in
our society is that we have constructed society in such a way that
some benefit at the expense of others, we can see that we can also
conceive of different economic systems and ways of relating.

In this book I have consistently maintained the notion of embodied religiosity; that we are not "spirits" seeking a nonearthly, non-
bodily home. We are not religious at the expense of our
embodiment, but through it. Nor does our set of beliefs and commitments as Christians separate us from the rest of the world in
such a way that we should worry about ourselves and let our neighbors worry about themselves. Quite the opposite! God's transforming grace is not directed only toward Christian insiders but toward
the entire world. The scope of God's grace directs churches to the
scope of their own action. Even if we actively wanted to separate

ourselves from the rest of the world, we are connected to it. We may separate ourselves from other human beings and live without dependence on their economic or political systems, although even this is increasingly difficult, given the dependence most of us have on the goods and services of others; but we cannot live without our animal and plant neighbors. The ecosystem cannot be divided as easily as we might separate from other human beings.

One of the reasons I appeal not just to the "memory" but also to the "presence" of Jesus is to point beyond the use of Jesus as mere "example." Jesus, so far as we can tell from the stories we have about him, was a person of his own time. This means, among other things, that we cannot expect the texts about Jesus to display the type of historical consciousness that we have attained only after the Enlightenment. No person of Jesus' time would have understood history as humanly constructed or seen the systemic causes of poverty or illness. We should not be surprised, then, that Jesus does not present a whole program for transforming the social and economic systems of his time. Yet Jesus also seems to have lived contextually. That is, stories show him responding to different situations with different solutions. Some need bodily healing; others need spiritual healing; still others need to sell some or all they have.

To appeal to the "presence" of Jesus in our own midst means to appeal not just to particular textual instances and examples (i.e., "memory"), but also to appeal to a recontextualizing of the meaning of Jesus for our time and place. Thus, now that we live in a time and place where we know that many of the impediments to flourishing and right relationship are humanly maintained and can be humanly altered, we cannot be satisfied with acts of charity that fail to look to the causes of the problems. Just because the biblical texts do not show Jesus as having a clear plan for political reform or for challenging the economic system does not mean that in his name we should not have such plans and make such challenges if such changes foster flourishing and right relationship.

If the task of churches is to foster flourishing and right relationship for all creation, they cannot depend only on biblical examples of laudable activity. They need to engage in serious contextual observation and analysis to understand the forces at play in the situations to which they turn themselves, for only attentive understanding of a context provides the necessary tools for understanding what needs to be done next.

For the last three to four decades, liberation theologies have arisen in a wide variety of contexts. One of the things such theologies have in common is articulating the difference between "being done to" and "having the tools to do for oneself." That is, if you want to know what is needed in a particular context, listen to those most affected to see how they understand what is happening. Liberation theologies point out that most theology and most decisions about action have been made by the powerful and privileged. In liberation theology the voice of the oppressed is crucial. One of the important tasks of a church seeking to act is listening to those with the least power and privilege. Much of the underlying philosophy of "mission" in the once-mainline churches has changed accordingly over these several decades. My own church, The United Church of Canada, for example, sends personnel to other areas of the world only when that is specifically requested, and then only to work in partnership with local people on a variety of tasks, not just the traditional work of staffing churches.

Also from liberation theology we need to understand and embrace the idea that theology is useless without action to change people's lives, not just temporarily, but over the long term. This means that churches and Christians need to understand economic forces. It means that we need to attend to how political systems work. It means that we need to see how systems tend to perpetuate themselves in favor of those who benefit.

We need to engage in systemic and systematic analysis. For all our supposed education in North America, few of us have really been educated in the art of "suspicion."[15] By suspicion I mean taking a given situation and asking about the forces in play that brought about the situation and sustain it without much change. I also mean asking whose interests are served by keeping things as they are. In part, it is difficult to carry out such an analytic task because most situations are complex, with the interplay of a host of forces, both historical and current. For example, the simplistic view of poverty in North America is that those who are poor choose poverty because they are too lazy to work. But such a view ignores a host of factors. For instance, why does poverty replicate itself? Why are the children of the poor often also poor? What is the link between poverty and access to and expectations of education? What is the link between hunger and ability to learn? How is a person's self-esteem affected by poverty? Why do we not guarantee a living income to all our citizens? Who benefits because the poor are poor? These are just a few of the questions that need to be asked before we might understand what positions to take on economic issues. The forces at play in any situation come from many different places; they are global, national, and local forces; they are forces from work, from home, from society. They are economic, political, social, ecclesiastical forces. Any given situation is complex, but its complexity should not be a reason for throwing up our hands in despair. We need to engage in whatever analysis we can to the best of our ability and draw on the resources we need to help in that analysis.

Although churches are resources for action, they should also not think that they are the only actors for social transformation. Although the motivations of those within churches might not be the same motivations for action as for those outside churches, there is much common cause that can be made with people of good will, who have a variety of religious and other commitments, in the interests of flourishing and right relationship. Flourishing and right relationship are not values that are unique to Christians; because the scope of action is global, alliances are both necessary and important. In Canada in the last couple of decades, various Christian denominations and often other religious groups and persons of good will have banded together to work on various social concerns. For instance, there is the Taskforce on the Churches and Corporate Responsibility and the Interchurch Committee on Human Rights in Latin America.[16] There is the Ten Days for World Development movement that each year picks a topic of social concern and provides groups with study and action materials. Such movements act as gathered bodies themselves and also provide congregations with educational resources and suggestions for their own analysis and action.

In response to drastic cuts in government services, which have a disproportionate negative effect on those who can least afford the cuts, the Sisters of Providence of St. Vincent de Paul in my area have organized a silent protest each Friday for more than two years. Each Friday, members of the order come with signs detailing the specific impact of the cuts and stand silently outside City Hall over the lunch hour. But they do not do this alone, for they have invited all the citizens who want to make the same protest to join them each week. The Sisters provide the structure and the organization for this orderly protest, but it is not a "Christian" protest. The people who come on Fridays are a diverse group in terms of class, occupation,

ethnic origin, sexual orientation, and religious commitment. What
unites these people is their opposition to the cuts to social spending
that make difficult lives even more difficult.

When church groups feel compelled to criticize government
action, as this group feels compelled to do in this particular case, it
means that they lose the cachet of being aligned with the halls of
governmental power. Although in an established democracy criticism of governments is an acceptable expression of opinion, still
churches and church groups might be reluctant to give up historic
status as part of the powerful in a given society.

Fostering flourishing and right relationship might at times call
for even more risky action. Congregations may have to be prepared
to be communities of resistance and to forge ties with other communities of resistance in actively seeking particular outcomes.
Critics of churches as institutions often point to the ways that historically the church has been an instrument of the status quo,
enforcing the way things are rather than actively seeking change.
Indeed, such a view of the church is well ingrained in the minds of
the undergraduate students I meet in my courses. They see the
church as a major force in opposing change, for example, in the status of women.

When they present themselves as arbiters of moral rules, and
when these rules serve to foster the status quo, churches are vehi-
cles for helping to control human action in particular ways. The
Roman Catholic Church's official stance on birth control is a good
example here. Even though the Roman Catholic Church claims
theological grounding for its stance, that theological grounding has
been questioned by many, both inside and outside that church. The
social effect of the Roman Catholic Church's stance is to make
women subject to unwanted pregnancies, and unwanted pregnancy
is clearly implicated in keeping women subordinate. When
churches promise an afterlife that will right all the wrongs of this
life without also trying to change this life for the vast majority of
people, they are sanctioning the status quo.

The risk that churches run is to lose the social respectability of
alliance with those in power. In Canada today, perhaps more than
in the United States, this alliance with power is shaky at best.
Whereas at the turn of the last century churches spoke to governments directly and governments often listened, today churches have
no direct "in" to governing. Although some of those in government

may be members of churches, the opinions of churches are set alongside other competing opinions (mostly those of business) for government attention. My point here is that in a complex and diverse society there are many competing voices, and churches cannot expect special audience or privilege. Thus, although churches might want to hark back to the "good old days" of influence, we are beyond those days in much of North America already. I am aware as I write this that in parts of the United States the link between churches and influence on government is much stronger than it is in Canada. Unless, however, we really are going to return to a kind of "Christian absolutism" in North America that assumes that all people are or should become Christians, we have to acknowledge the legitimacy of a variety of voices to be heard.

I think that churches gain credibility by not being allied too closely with government or with any other social power. Churches need to be free agents in the realm of commentary on social and political matters, analyzing contexts with seriousness and advocating approaches consonant with the transforming grace of God, without worrying about upsetting the powers that be. My own contention is that such a stance would give churches far more credibility with religious seekers today than the former alliances with power have done. Again, it is a matter of sanctioning the struggle with difficult issues rather than sanctioning a single "rule" for action.

A church that does not know all the rules for social action will to a certain extent be destabilized. Different contexts may call for completely different responses even if, superficially, the issue looks the same. The solution to the problem of vast numbers of homeless in a large urban area may be very different from the solutions in a predominantly rural area. Much more emphasis will need to be placed on discernment, and local and national churches may not always agree on what is called for. Churches that engage in serious discussion and discernment around points of view and outcomes take the risk of not always being "right." Churches give up certitude for life as lived.

What can people in a local congregation do? They can study the problems and their own contextual realities. They can protest the actions of local and larger governments when these actions cut off flourishing and right relationship for many. They can challenge the common interpretations of the problems. They can make alliances with others who have similar concerns. They can refuse to engage in congregational practices that reinscribe rather than change oppressions.

The work of churches in the world is to continue the work of eros, of intimate relationship both within its walls and beyond its own boundaries, to encompass the universe.

NOTES

1. See, for example, Nancy Tatom Ammerman, with Arthur E. Farnsley II et al., *Congregation and Community* (New Brunswick: Rutgers University Press, 1997), 349ff.

2. See ibid., 351–52; and Elizabeth Bounds, *Coming Together/ Coming Apart: Religion, Community and Modernity* (New York: Routledge, 1997), 4–5.

3. The common uses of community listed here and referred to in the following pages are from Bounds, *Coming Together/ Coming Apart*, 2.

4. Sharon Welch, *Communities of Resistance and Solidarity* (Maryknoll, N.Y.: Orbis Books, 1985).

5. Letty Russell, *Church in the Round: Feminist Interpretation of the Church* (Louisville: Westminster/John Knox, 1993), 46–74.

6. Douglas Ottati, "Recovering Faithfulness in Our Callings," in Gabriel O'Donnell and Robin Maas, eds., *Spiritual Traditions for the Contemporary Church* (Nashville: Abingdon, 1990), 228ff.

7. Margaret Ruth Miles, *Practicing Christianity: Critical Perspectives for an Embodied Spirituality* (New York: Crossroad, 1988), 190.

8. Ibid., 91.

9. Ibid., 126.

10. Ibid., 131.

11. For a helpful summary of Ignatian spirituality, see Barbara Bedolla and Dominic Totaro, "Ignatian Spirituality," in O'Donnell and Maas, eds., *Spiritual Traditions for the Contemporary Church*, 171–88.

12. John P. McIntyre, "Accountability Before God: The Examen," in O'Donnell and Maas, eds., *Spiritual Traditions for the Contemporary Church*, 197.

13. Miles, *Practicing Christianity*, 143.

14. Chalmers United Church is located in Kingston, Ontario, Canada.

15. This word, first used by Paul Ricoeur, is widely used in liberation theologies.

16. For a good overview of the work of many of these coalitions, see Christopher Lind and Joe Mihevc, eds., *Coalitions for Justice: The Story of Canada's Interchurch Coalitions* (Ottawa: Novalis, 1994).

Conclusion

It is difficult for people to find any community, let alone a religious community, that might support their growth and development as human beings. Religious searches for meaning and value and purpose often do not find where the search ends successfully. As I have argued in this book, churches could be communities that have both the symbolic means to help people struggle with important questions and the resources to embody and communicate those means. That they often do not succeed in meeting human religious needs at the turn of the millennium is a function both of those inside and those outside the church. Those inside need to turn their attention beyond the mere perpetuation of what has been to the question of what might be, and searchers need to engage in a similar task. Instead of spurning what is because it does go far enough, they too might think in terms of what might be. They could be co-creators of making the possibilities more real.

Some within churches will read this book as though what I am asking is that churches should capitulate to the world and become just one more set of organizations trying to discover what the market is so they can design a product to fit the market or create a need that only their product can fill. I am not intending to portray churches as just more mass producers of products for consumption. Churches cannot and should not be all things to all people. Moreover, in light of the source of their identity, there are boundaries to what churches can be.

One can take seriously the importance of context without capitulating the Christian churches' identity in the gospel of Jesus Christ. Just because the Christian church has a history of two thousand years, this does not mean that it needs to be as outdated and irrelevant as it often appears to be. One can live in, and be relevant to, one's own time and place while still being critical, if necessary, of the dominant themes or values of that time and place. Churches have to learn how to articulate the gospel in their own contexts.

In *Congregation and Community*, a study of a variety of congregations in the United States that have adapted to change in a host of ways, Nancy Ammerman discovered that not all churches have the same mission.

> [Congregations] are neither the "lifestyle enclaves" of individualistic religious consumers nor traditionalistic throwbacks to an earlier time. They are social creations of the modern world, encompassing the both/and quality of modern social life, not an either/or accommodation. They are gatherings of individuals who choose to be there. Where religious identities are not fundamentally ascribed, individual choice is fundamental to congregational life. In this system of choice (and the pluralism it implies) congregations are thoroughly modern institutions. Yet they are communal gatherings, collectivities, that afford their members an opportunity for connections with persons, groups, divine powers, and social structures beyond their own individuality.[1]

The issue does arise of how the churches might communicate to a world that tends not to believe in their relevance. A single church cannot be all things to all people. Churches need to proclaim their identities and their diversities better than they seem to have been doing. I noted in a recent newspaper article that some Canadian religious orders were starting to use advertising agencies to proclaim that they have changed with the times. Churches need to think about how to proclaim their identities within their communities. This may not entail hiring an advertising agency to "market" them, but it certainly does mean that they need to think about how they present themselves. Thus, through advertising, press coverage, word of mouth, events sponsored by the church, and so on, the message of that church's particular identity needs to be communicated. We no longer live in an age where people are automatically looking for a church (or religious) home, so churches must look at the question of why someone would choose a particular church. Ammerman's study of various congregations shows that some congregations can and do change and adapt to their contexts.[2] Change is possible if the will is there to change. The locus of change to meet changed circumstances is primarily in the congregation rather than in the wider church structures. Vital communities read the signs of the times and figure out how to respond to them.

The number of members is not everything. Churches need resources to accomplish their tasks, but growth (or its alternative, fear of demise) does not need to be the primary concern. A congregation that has a clear mission (or cluster of missions) and is seeking to live it out may not grow by leaps and bounds, but it will be able to live with integrity vis-à-vis the gospel and the world.

I have waited until the conclusion of this book to talk about the traditional marks of the church: one, holy, catholic, and apostolic. I have puzzled over these "marks" as I have been writing. The more I puzzled, the less certain I became about their usefulness. Sometimes I have talked about "the church." But even as I have done so, I have been painfully aware that "the church" I envisage bears little resemblance to "the church" envisaged by much of the tradition. I have even begun to wonder whether there is a "the church." In the ecumenical movement of the mid-twentieth century, most of us hoped, I think, for the end to denominationalism, hoped that we could overcome divisions of theology and authority to reunite the church so that it could truly be "one." But at what price would this "oneness" be bought? I could not conceive of belonging to a church that would not ordain women or would not organize itself into relatively democratic decision making that would give voice to all within it, ordered or not. There are compromises I would not make for unity. Furthermore, the kind of unity that might be achieved would seem to be achieved at the expense of contextuality, of taking peoples' everyday lives and concerns seriously as different from time to time and place to place. Thus I am not at all sure that, even as an ideal, I would espouse the unity of the church if it meant glossing over the diversities of the churches.

Perhaps, then, we could see the unity of the church inherent in its gospel rather than in itself. But the gospel also comes in many forms and many interpretations. Whatever the gospel is conceived to be, appeal to its authority takes many different forms. In this book, when I have written of the shared memory and presence of Jesus Christ, I hope that others will resonate with my interpretation of this shared memory and presence in such a way that it can animate their own religious and ecclesial lives. But I am cognizant that, as responsible as I have tried to be to the sources and traditions as I understand them, there are competing interpretations. The unity of the church can be said, I think, to reside in Jesus Christ. But, that said, there are many different interpretations of Jesus Christ that arise.

The church is said to be "holy." But it is also generally acknowledged that the visible church is subject to sin and temptation. Holiness might function as an ideal. If I were to explore holiness as an ideal, I would speak of it in the terms in which I talked about the church's task of "seeking to embody God's transforming grace by fostering flourishing and right relationship for all creation." The visible church is manifestly not "holy," although it might strive to be so.

We are in a religiously plural world where many Christians have come to recognize that the church is not the only way to be religious. Some Christians, myself included, although we claim truth, goodness, and beauty for Christianity, are not willing or able to say that Christianity is the only or even the best religious way.[3] Thus I would not see the church as catholic or universal in the sense of needing to draw all others in, either to the church visible or to some view of the church invisible. God's grace encompasses the whole world, and the grace of Jesus Christ that inspires and enlivens the church is the same grace of God that is available always and everywhere. But the danger in emphasizing the universality of the church is that we are inevitably brought into an "inclusivist" view of the religious world that tries to embrace all other religious ways under Christianity and argues that Christianity is the best or fullest way.

Christianity is a particular way of being religious. It is only one way. It is, I think, at least in its most healthy forms, a good way of being religious that tells the truth about the universe and ourselves in it. But I do not see the church as encompassing the whole world. I am unwilling to universalize one particular historical religious view as though it included everyone. Thus I find less and less need for a notion of "invisible church" that is broad enough to encompass all persons of good will regardless of religious affiliation. So I do not think that the idea of the catholicity of the church holds up well as a desideratum.

As "apostolic," the church strives to adhere to the witness of the apostles. I do not think that there is any guarantee of apostolicity, such as an unbroken line of apostolic succession. If the church is apostolic, it is so only more or less as it lives out its faithfulness to the apostolic witness to Jesus Christ.

The church is not coextensive with the world. It is a diverse collection of ways of being in the world. Through continuing to simply pass on the "marks" of the church, albeit with commentary that offers caveats at all stages, we gloss over the very real historical changes and differences that have challenged the church over time.[4]

Churches have much to offer to those who are looking. Historical communities have persisted over two thousand years. Many within them have found them life-giving. Many have found in the figure of Jesus Christ someone through whom they can understand what it means to be human and how we should relate to God and the rest of the universe. But churches are not automatically life-giving. Nor can they rest on past laurels or traditions. Churches must be continually remaking themselves to rise to the challenges of living the gospel in each time and place. Only then can they be places where one might expect to find flourishing and right relationship—where eros connects us to God, to self, and to all others in the universe.

NOTES

1. Nancy Tatom Ammerman, with Arthur E. Farnsley II et al., *Congregation and Community* (New Brunswick: Rutgers University Press, 1997), 352.

2. Ammerman, *Congregation and Community*.

3. See my *Christ in a Post-Christian World: How Can We Believe in Jesus Christ When Those Around Us Believe Differently—or Not at All?* (Minneapolis: Fortress, 1995).

4. For a good overview of the doctrine of the church, see Peter C. Hodgson and Robert C. Williams, "The Church," in Peter C. Hodgson and Robert H. King, eds., *Christian Theology: An Introduction to Its Traditions and Tasks*, second edition (Minneapolis: Fortress, 1994), 249–73.

Index